Sustaining Lean

How to develop principles and practices
for creating a self sustaining Lean Organisation

John HURST

2010

John Hurst, Author.
ISBN 978-1-4461-7897-3

Foreword

Having been involved in organising and running many Lean Tools workshops, I can unequivocally say that they never fail to bring results. The size of the results depends on the knowledge and ability of the organisers and the openness and willingness of the company to implement changes.

Having also been a Works Manager of a plant struggling with the implementation of lean tools, I can also say that sustainability after the workshop is incredibly difficult!

In the early days of General Motors Europe's efforts to introduce lean, I remember Masaki Imai, author of the book "Kaizen" (consulting for GME at the time), saying that people involvement is the key to leveraging the results. Management can not do it alone.

To help us understand the various approaches to Kaizen, the Kaizen Institute organised a fact finding trip to Japan, during which we visited many companies including service industry (airline), component machining and manufacturing, press plants and product assembly (including vehicles).

Each of these companies had their particular focus i.e. Total Quality Management, Just in Time, or Total Productive Maintenance as their lead activity, but they all demonstrated the same level of commitment and involvement from their workforce.

Contrasts with western practices were highlighted in all the companies we visited.

For example in the component machining company, the machines were all 30+ years old, but in terms of their condition all looked brand new. They were spotless, with no sign of oil leakage on or around the machines. There were no signs of paint chips. All air, coolant and lubrication pipes were neatly attached to the machines with no sign of degradation. There were labels attached to some machines : these were put in place by production operators from their equipment check, asking maintenance to correct a substandard condition.

Many western companies consider machines to be old after 10 years ; the approach in this company was to improve the machines over many years, to be better than the original design parameters.

Time and time again it was stressed: "your people know more about the production processes than management; therefore they must be fully involved in the improvement activities".

Observing their activities, it looked pretty straight forward!

Our various attempts to involve people as participants in workshops met with mixed results but did nothing for the sustainability of improvements or for the continuation of making improvements.

Some areas managed impressive improvements, where others made very modest gains ; both would have been completely acceptable if incremental improvements had continued.

But alas it was not so, some incredibly important ingredient was missing.

In contrast to this, when I took a three year assignment on at Toyota UK Burnaston I discovered that improvement was a daily expectation and reality.

Every member of the workforce was expected to carry out improvements on his operation coached by the team leader.

In all aspects of the work place performance (safety, quality, delivery, cost, and human development) there were improvement activities identified and being carried out on almost a daily basis.

Although these activities were management initiated from the business plan, they were driven by the teams and groups.

The management team took on the role of reviewing progress, coaching to resolve difficulties, supporting activities and giving recognition.

The process used for operation improvement is identified in this book along with the many practices that will encourage your workforce to play a positive role.

Why was it so different?

The age old answer that Japanese people are different to western Europeans did not stand up. The employees in Burnaston were predominantly western European the same as in the other manufacturers in the UK.

Also the argument that it can only happen in greenfield sites is not true. When Taiichi Ohno started the change to Just In Time production he was dealing with existing plants using mass production techniques.

It was the poor reputation internationally of the Japanese industries that acted as the catalyst for improvement. Their determination to change and become world leaders was the catalyst, the rest as they say is history!

It is clear to me that there is a big difference in the relationship between the company and its employees. Trust plays a big part, a trust that is jealously guarded by the management team.

The way in which the company operates, its organisation, behaviours, practices and reward system all focus the entire workforce on the business needs, particularly as there is a direct link with the needs of the workforce.

People involvement is much more than participating in workshops. It is also having a say in the daily work routine, and it is being empowered to change what is not working properly.

It is this and much more as you will discover in this book.

Lean tools/techniques are just the tip of the iceberg. Beneath the water level is a whole story about business fundamentals, organisation structure, behaviours and practices that focus on the needs of the business.

Although the Toyota approach may not be the answer for everyone, the more that you can adopt and adapt from this book, the better your chances of levering your bottom line results.

I have endeavoured to explain as clearly as possible what is required to attain sustainability. The descriptions and aids for implementation are deliberately simple. There is no need to make things complicated when they can be simple and easy to apply, so if those supplied still look too complicated, feel free to simplify!

This is not just about techniques to apply; there are fundamental issues to work through, because without resolving them you will never capture the potential improvement available through your workforce.

At the end of each chapter I have included actions to help you determine how you can implement changes.

If the world wide financial crisis has taught us anything, it is that things get done when we all work together, hopefully we do not have to wait for another crisis to start that process of coming closer together.

I wish you good reading and lots of success in your efforts.

Contents

III. « Really « Involving People   89

Introduction

2008 and 2009 have been disastrous years for the Business Community and industry. It has been painful watching the demise of General Motors and Chrysler as they have been forced to file for bankruptcy protection, downsize, and negotiate salary packages at a more competitive level.

Although it is clear that the world wide financial crisis was caused by Financial Institutions not Industry, it is never less manufacturing companies and their workers who will suffer far longer than anyone else before things are put right.

Every type of manufacturer has been affected to one degree or another with plunging demand literally drying the market up for house builders, appliance manufacturers, the aero-industry etc.

For the big players in the auto-industry the crisis only accelerated their demise.GM and Chrysler were already dying a death of a thousand cuts, even without the financial crisis.

Compared to Toyota their operations were very inefficient. They were over-investing in their plants and equipment and both had too many plants. For GM, this was also true in Europe.

On the other hand Toyota has always invested in equipment conservatively while developing equipment through their technical and maintenance departments. "Low cost and simple" has been their by-word for many years.
Even so, they have suffered in this crisis, having to lay off thousands of temporary workers and implementing short time working.

Coincidentally having just achieved number one in auto-sales worldwide, they also experienced the worst quality spill in their history. Typical of Toyota they have not gone into denial, they are revisiting their well know quality basics and putting in place a global quality team to oversee their customer quality systems.

Due to their diversity of product and their lower cost base they remain poised ready to lead the charge as things improve.

There is still much to learn from the Japanese approach to manufacturing and in particular Toyota which is applicable to all sorts of business.
That is not to say there are no other companies out there doing well, but after 20 years as a leading manufacturer, who has developed very powerful lean tools, available to the world, it would be crazy not to take the opportunity to continue to learn from Toyota.

Why it is important to continue to learn from Toyota after the financial crisis

As early as the 80s & 90s it was clear to everyone in the automotive industry that there were too many manufacturing plants world wide (volume greater than demand), and inevitably one or more of the companies was going to have to rationalise if they did not want to be losers.

Toyota with its Just In Time (JIT) production system was leading the world in quality and cost, and although not yet one of the big three, was considered to be the "world class" manufacturer of automobiles.

Toyota began its cost reduction activities by focusing on first time quality, ensuring that the product delivered to its customers was of the highest standard in terms of delivered quality and reliability.

Taiichi Ohno, Toyota's great pioneer of JIT production had realised how much mass production drives up the cost of producing, as well as creating huge stocks of vehicles that no one wants to buy.

The Japanese market although not huge was very demanding in the variation of product. Ohno realised that to plan a month's production required predicting what the customer would want. When he compared this to a supermarket replenishment system he realised that Just in Time production replenishing popular models would be far more effective.

Under his guidance they soon progressed to driving out all forms of waste, by adopting Just in Time production principles and small lots strategy.

Although Quality plays the key role in production, Toyota has nevertheless put great stress on driving out all forms of waste, and emphasising the concept of value added work to achieve continuous cost reduction as the way to remain competitive.

In 1990 ***The Machine That Changed The World*** a book co-written by Jim Womack, Dan Jones and Daniel Roos (following a five year, $5million study on the future of the Auto-industry by The Massachusetts Institute of Technology), came to the conclusion that Japanese industry and in particular Toyota was beginning to lead the world, a fact that was well known within the industry during the latter part of the 1980s.

This led many of the major manufacturing companies to introduce lean tools as stand alone techniques to improve performance; 5S, Kaizen, Total Productive Maintenance and Practical Problem Solving to name just a few. But as the focus was inevitably on the techniques applied to the tools, sustaining the improvements proved to be very difficult when focus moved to numerous new projects.

Needless to say the workforce saw this as "flavour of the month" and dropped the previous activity as they move to the next.

During my years at General Motors Europe considerable effort was made to implement lean practices, we discovered that when starting a "Greenfield"* site, lean practices were readily accepted by the workforce and Trade Unions. However implementing change in existing plants was fraught with many difficulties, particularly as the company had well established behavioural practices that did not fit with lean production.

Even though in 1994 GME started to hire ex Toyota/Nissan people to work directly in the plants to be able to give daily assistance in the application of lean tools, it is my belief that GM has still not understood the importance of the underlying philosophy and practices.
These bind the tools into more than "lean practices" or a "production system", but into a "culture of challenge" continuously striving for improvement at all levels of the organisation.

On retiring from General Motors I had the opportunity to work for Toyota as a production manager for the following three years.

I experienced differences that even though I had studied the Toyota Production System for more than a decade, completely surprised me, not only in its application, but also because of its simplicity.

Greenfield site is a newly constructed plant with new employees and therefore no existing culture/ company agreements to change.

The following is just one example of the underlying philosophical and practice differences:

In GM car assembly plants, state of the art equipment was installed to lift brake pipe and fuel line assemblies and fix them automatically to the under body. The equipment was very sophisticated and used control systems that the UK maintenance teams were not familiar with.
No expense was spared to train all of the maintenance in trouble shooting this equipment. They gamely struggled on for months on end until they started to develop the skills and experience needed.

However when I went to Toyota I discovered very simple equipment including an Automated Guided Vehicle which offered up the brake pipes and fuel lines, which had been designed and manufactured by the shop kaizen team.

Where GM was investing in advanced technology and training to keep up with technical changes, Toyota on the other hand was minimising investment while developing the skills and knowledge of its workforce to be able to improve and modify its equipment at low cost.

This is just one example but in fact I discovered many differences in the philosophy and practices between the two companies, even for activities that were called by the same name!

I also experienced how Toyota operates to its Beliefs and values (called Toyota Way) treating its workforce in a very dignified manner, while at the same time driving change and improvement on a daily basis.

Daily improvement activities are written into the terms and conditions of employment, but this is reinforced by an industry competitive benefits package and a bonus system agreed annually for when targets are met.

Hidden Facets of The Toyota Production System

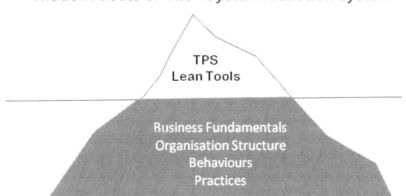

The diagram above (Fig.1) shows the facets of the Toyota business model that get totally overlooked by its competitors; these are the basics that make the lean tools so powerful. These are all covered in this book.

Their engagement process provides a dynamic activity that engages the full workforce; managers, support groups and shop floor personnel working together in an environment that allows the members to manage their own activities, thus making decisions that in a traditional organisation would be left to management to decide and implement.

It provides an organisation that will not stand back and watch others fail but where everyone has input and therefore a stake in the success of activities.

If you wish to gain the same benefits, you will have to pay as much attention to developing a "Company Culture", that promotes the same kind of action and re-action.

This requires putting focus on the hidden facets of the Toyota Production System, developing a proper understanding of business fundamentals and how to structure and develop the organisation to think and act differently.

The key however is going to be whether your workforce and the trade union feel and act like partners in the company, and whether the management team will develop a different relationship with them born out of respect for the different perspectives they bring.

There is nothing wrong with the workforce/ Trade Union having a slightly different perspective, as long as everyone can see that the business needs of the company must take priority over dogma and politics. For this to work however, the success of the company must result in positive impact on the workforce, e.g. cost savings must be shared through a bonus system.

If goals are not achieved though, for whatever reason, the bonus should only be paid proportional to the actual cost savings achieved.

This is important to grasp because historically in many mass producing companies the bonus has been paid irrespective of real bottom line performance. Blame for performance being placed on management practices or lack of sales by the sales department etc!! This disconnects the workforce from the success of the company and must be resisted at all costs!

The protection of jobs at all costs must be replaced with flexible working and a permanent workforce sized to suit the ability of the company to support them in the long term while making a profit.

Following all of these changes, getting the right approach to Production systems and the means for Continuous Improvement will finally begin to have real meaning.

Now more than ever using a low cost just in time approach to manufacturing products is very important because the gap can be closed!

This book has been developed from my perception of how Toyota has managed to develop its improvement culture and create sustainability through the involvement of its workforce.

It has been written to stimulate those with the will to develop their own way of achieving the same condition or culture.

It is important to recognise that this is not just a formula to be applied, that developing your own "Lean Company Culture" is what will bring success.

It must also be stated that this book is not **just** applicable to the auto industry or even industry; it also has applications in retail and service, in fact for **_all_** organisations large and small!!

The same principles apply to all companies that have managed to avoid collapse, as they climb back out of the recession new thinking must be applied to the way they do business not only with the customer but with their own workforce.

If you want sustainable competitiveness the biggest change must come from how the total workforce thinks, from managing director to the worker on the shop floor.

The Lean Tools are a collection of principles and techniques which can be learned easily by anyone through the use of the many seminars, public workshops and practice.

They are after all only a collection of best practices from Industrial Engineering, Quality Assurance and Maintenance, repackaged in such a way that they can be applied not by specialist engineers but by a well trained workforce.

There are hundreds and thousands of consultant companies just ready to relieve you of some of your hard earned cash to help you with the techniques if you really can't understand them.

But before you spend all that money, look into your organisation, you may have all the consultants you need, engineers who plan your processes, engineers and maintenance men who design and maintain your equipment, quality engineers who quantify your quality requirements and last but not least the *"consultants"* who carry out the manufacturing processes for you.

Between them they can share the work, the operators as discoverers of potential problems, the engineers as specialist support for technical issues and management supplying resources and training.

Who knows reality better

than them?

A more cost effective way to learn the tools may be:

1. Identify key support people (process designers, engineers, maintenance engineers and quality engineers) and send them on some of the public hands on workshops on lean tools along with top and middle management. In these workshops they will learn how to apply the well established practices through the workforce instead of specialist departments.

2. Provide them with the latest guides to implementation *(a list of useful technical books on lean tools is provided at the back of this book).*

3. Then work with them to develop your production system and the systematic use of the lean tools. (*Focussing on how to use the tools as daily improvement activities which engage the workforce in cross functional activities)*

4. For those tools you need additional support for, approach consultancies for specific assistance, but keep control of implementation yourselves. Alternatively hire a senior manager with experience of lean manufacturing.

Frankly it is not the application of the tools that will frustrate your efforts; in fact as long as you have the focus on lean, the tools have been proved to work over and over again.

The real problem is going to be how you get managers, supervisors, workers and trade unions to embrace them. This must start from top down, by engaging your management team and subject specialists, as they learn about the concepts; they will be able to develop your own production system principles as a frame work within which to apply the improvement tools. For this process it will be necessary to train the leaders of your trade union with your managers allowing them input at the planning stage sooner than just as you start to implement.

Managers and group leaders will be able to determine the appropriate Key Performance Indicators to measure progress and keep on track. They will also be able to train the workforce in the application of the tools, thus demonstrating their understanding and commitment to the new production principles.

By using the Lean Tools you will learn that the only sustainable way to increase profit is by reducing costs:

Selling Price – Cost = Profit

By applying lean principles and using the lean tools you must change the thinking in the organisation away from "mass production thinking" to:

"Lean Thinking"

Small lot size, surfacing problems sooner than hiding them, and eliminating all forms of waste wherever it is found.

All types of waste can be found in great quantities in all businesses large and small. They can be eliminated by a well trained, knowledgeable workforce. But eliminating them in large enough quantities and in a manner that ensures they remain eliminated takes a different approach to the business partnership.

This approach and the consequent behaviours and practices are covered in this book; it is my intention to go into depth, with a practical in the work place approach, to show why Japanese companies are successful in making lean practices sustainable.

This book should be used as a guideline as to how your company could implement changes in its practices and behaviours to induce a culture of continuous improvement with sustained commitment.

I am going to identify and explain the three basic requirements that need to be considered when trying to make the change to lean; those requirements are shown in figure 2 opposite.

Engaging The Workforce

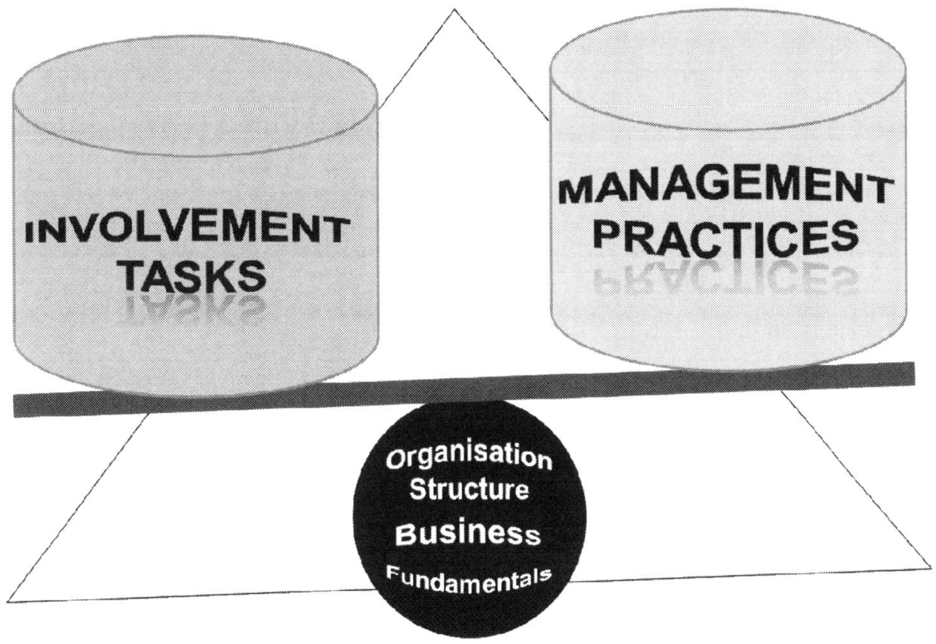

Fig. 2

I will give practical hints and guidance to assist you and will identify actions that you should engage your self in to make this more than a reading exercise.

Perhaps not all will be achievable in every organisation, but it should stimulate your thinking about what you can achieve and how to go about it.

In part I, I will explain The Importance of Business Fundamentals and having a Lean Organisation structure and will develop both subjects with examples.

In part II, we will look at Management Practices that support the involvement and development of the work force, examining management involvement & support activities and how to lead not manage, and we will also identify the important aspects of the role of the front line supervisor in a lean organisation.

In part III, I will define how to really involve the workforce in a practical, business focused manner which allows opportunities for personal and team development.

I. Setting the Right Environment

If your aim is to have an organisation that is fully involved in making the company a success, then an open and collaborative environment is needed to encourage and make practical this concept of workforce involvement.

Two basic elements are required for setting this environment; first the workforce must be fully informed and understand what the business is all about (business fundamentals). The workforce not only needs to understand that this is a widget making company, but will it develop into other products over time, or will the focus be on increasing current sales volumes and increasing efficiency?

What developments are taking place in the industry and how will they affect the company?

Will new technology development be important?

Will the company need to improve its current production system?

What does all this mean to us?

Do we have to change?

How will we do it?

How will we know if we are succeeding?

All of these questions must be answered to create the business fundamentals that will drive everything that happens within the company.

Second, getting the balance of the organisation right will help lower the decision making level in the company encouraging the workforce to participate and make decisions. With the right organisational structure, a matrix management approach can be developed, where various departments will collaborate, sharing resources and creating high levels of synergy.

Let's start by looking at what we mean by Business Fundamentals.

1. Business Fundamentals

"World Class Organisations generally are those that know where they are going and how they intend to get there.

They have a clear vision of what their company will look like in the next 3-5 years and what it will take to make them successful.

Future plant size, headcount, product line up, competitive position and methods and practices to get there are all part of the vision.

They will have converted that vision into practical objectives that must be achieved by all departments such that the puzzle all fits together and complements each other in a way that the whole is greater than the sum of the parts".

The following 5 items make up the business fundamentals of any company. Without defining them clearly, it will be difficult, if not impossible, to explain to your workforce how the success of the company can be achieved and provide mutual benefits for all stake holders.

Create a Vision of the future for the Company.

- Company performance versus competitors.

- Operating (production) principles & system.

- Business Plan Deployment process.

- Creating mutual benefit.

- Beliefs, Values & Supporting Behaviours of the company.

When creating a vision of the future state of the company, it is important to be clear about the state of the business today versus competition and where you want to be in the next 3 -5years.

You should describe the operating (production) system you will utilise to get to your vision. Identify the tools to be applied to improving costs on a regular basis and the rules for applying them.

Identity the systemised process you will use to ensure you stay on track to achieve your 3 -5 year goals, through good annual business plan deployment and focussed tracking.

You must develop a working relationship with the workforce built on business needs, avoiding confrontational management styles and politics. Creating terms, conditions and mutual benefits that encourages the desire to continuously improve performance.

Finally, the vision must include the fundamental beliefs and values that the company will operate under in order to develop a strong challenging environment, where everybody can have input and receive benefit from their efforts.

Let us take these items one at a time and determine what needs to be done:

Understanding Company Performance

Does everyone understand the state of the company and its standing within the industry?

Who are its main competitors and what is the potential in the market place today?

What are the risks the company currently faces and how great are they?

What does the company do in terms of being a good civic partner within the community?

If your employees do not understand the state of the business and how they can positively impact it, you can't possibly expect them to enthusiastically support improvement activities.

Educating your workforce must be the starting point for changing employee's perceptions and beginning the process of engagement.

Regular communication is required to update and help the workforce become part of the team.

Do not settle for awareness packages but seek to increase the knowledge and understanding of your employees, by demonstrating performance linkage to the bottom line and therefore the competitiveness of the company.

Awareness and knowledge create interest, but only a developed understanding will start the process of attaining commitment.

To set the right environment for the change to Lean Manufacturing it is important to create an understanding of why change is needed. It is not sufficient to just say "to be competitive".

Your vision should reflect the gap between where you are and where you need to be. The vision should be factual, utilising key performance indicators in the *key areas of:* Safety, Quality, Cost, Delivery and HR development (plus other indicators such as annual sales, customer requirements, product development etc as required).

Having established this clear vision with goals, objectives and annual targets, it is necessary to be clear what is wrong with the way the company is operating today. Therefore what it will take to move the company in the direction that will enable it to grow to its full potential.

As a minimum requirement, companies coming out of this global crisis should realise it is important for them not to go back to where they were before the collapse. As demand increases it is imperative that the vision of the workforce size is determined based on anticipated demand levels, allied to good process design practices.

Temporary labour should be employed to cushion foreseen fluctuations and overtime should be considered to manage demand peaks (see page 29 for how world class companies manage this).

To minimise costs every process should be compared to the required standard of zero waste and as near to 95% loading as possible. Kaizen activities should be carried out coupled to line re-balancing to achieve this requirement.

Only after you have thoroughly kaizened*, balanced the processes, and decided how to manage fluctuations and peaks should you consider re-hiring, as your commitment to your workforce must preclude hiring & firing!
Kaizen : to continuously improve your business activities.

To enlarge the vision let us now review the type of production system that will enable you to maximise your efforts.

Operating (production) Principles & System.

The new practices which will move your company towards world class should hinge around "Lean Production System" principles and tools so generously developed by Toyota, which are well known throughout industry and still applicable today.

Your vision should identify how your Production System will operate;

A small lot production activity (JIT = lot size of one)

Focus on the elimination of all forms of waste.

Continuous cost reduction activities to improve profits.

The production tools and standards should be identified and your expectations of the workforce clearly spelt out.

Toyota for example utilise Just In Time (JIT) as their production principles and they have established rules on lot size, first time quality, inventory size, cost reduction, sizes of buffers, etc. and have identified the "Lean Tools" as the methodology to achieve cost reduction targets.

They fully expect that these rules will show up deficiencies in equipment performance, process design, people's skills and abilities, internal systems and even supplier performance.

These are seen as opportunities to improve and therefore make cost reductions; they are not seen as opportunities to blame people for problems.

Many companies sit on the fence between mass production and JIT using the TPS tools without such guidelines and fail to make savings of the same magnitude as Toyota.

This is not surprising as the tools are designed for maximum effect in a JIT environment.

Toyota sees the journey to JIT as a long term objective and every kaizen undertaken moves them closer to that goal.

Those who try to emulate TPS give up on JIT because it seems to be too difficult to achieve immediately. Initially their facilities do not operate at sufficiently high uptime rates, so fear stops them from applying JIT principles in case they get blamed for shortfalls.

The secret is to apply the principles and use lean tools to reduce the downtime and improve quality coming ever closer to one piece flow with zero buffers.

Think of the problems uncovered as nuggets of gold to be converted to your benefit; many are as easy to convert as picking the nuggets off the ground.

Hiding behind huge buffers prevents improvement and cost reduction and therefore insidiously eats away at your profits.

Thank people for uncovering the problems and praise them for solving them.

Do not blame them for causing them and do not take it for granted that they will be fixed!

"Toyota is not at the point of achieving pure JIT yet, so don't give up or you will lose considerable improvement potential.

Think of JIT as an end point that each improvement must take you one step closer to".

You may never achieve pure JIT production but you will save huge amounts of money by trying!

I have no intention of going into great detail on the "lean tools" (except where they support the subject matter of this book) as there are many books published that cover them well enough, I have however included in the back of this book a list of the tools and some of the books available.

World class companies understand that linking Just in Time (small lot) principles to lean tools is the key to the *magnitude of improvement* you are likely to make.

Continuing to think with mass production logic e.g. inventory and buffers being used to mask poor equipment performance will not enable you to make large cost reductions.

Likewise there is a natural order to implementing lean based on;

Make the situation clear (current condition objectives, targets).

Eliminate as much waste as possible and establish standards from which improvement can be made.

Carry out improvements and re-establish the standard.

Formalise improvement methods.

It is surprising how many companies that try to go lean move directly to trying to eliminate waste without understanding the current condition.

This means they do not understand what they are trying to achieve and how far away from it they are.

A simple example is trying to improve processes in a workshop that has poor Workplace Organisation (5S) conditions.

How can they tell what is meant to be where?

Is there stability in the shop layout and conditions?

The reality is that they are trying to improve a continuously changing condition. Therefore as much as they try to eliminate waste, it will creep back and negate the improvements gained.

Not all of the tools will have the same impact in all manufacturing shops, so it is very important to first understand the type of processing required e.g. batch vs one piece flow, or equipment intensive vs people intensive. By doing this you can decide the best tools to utilise in each shop to maximise the required cost reduction or profit attainment.

For example in a workplace that is heavily equipment biased, using lean tools such as Bottleneck Management, Problem Solving, Standardisation, Total Productive Maintenance and Single Minute Exchange of Dies (quick change over) will create benefits quicker than some of the other lean tools.

A word of caution : in this kind of activity it is best to start improvements using bottleneck management to understand the true bottleneck equipment in the workshop. Target them for first attention using TPM, problem solving and SMED etc. to improve their performance thus creating a new bottleneck to work on.

As this happens your savings from the first bottleneck will go immediately to the bottom line, whereas if you had worked on a random piece of equipment it would have had no effect on your bottom line.

Continue with the bottleneck approach to spread out the new practices, in this way making savings as you learn.

This is why the vision and the methodology of achieving it is of prime importance just as knowing where you are going and how to drive is important when you get into your automobile in the morning!

Having established a clear vision, complete with a defined Operating System and with goals, objectives and annual targets, it is necessary to have a process with which you can deploy them and establish plans at the working level to achieve them.

This process in world Class companies is called Business Plan Deployment.

Business Plan Deployment

In the majority of traditional companies cost reduction efforts are focussed on managing the financial budget. The budget is established by the finance department and annual targets are normally set on a % reduction of the previous year's actual costs.

The targets are normally given to the manager of the department broken down by expense account so that he can communicate to his supervisory team how much they must save from each.

The focus is then normally on management control of expenditure sooner than finding more effective ways to perform. Headcount reduction is normally only as good as the turnover of labour and the departments with attrition have to find ways to cope without the labour.

World Class Companies utilise an activity called Business Plan Deployment to create a process of involving the total workforce in achieving the Master plan, through a series of connected practical and achievable mini plans worked out by the people at the working level.

In order for a company to achieve its vision it must have concrete goals, specific objectives, clear and measurable targets understood by everyone, and a practical methodology for achieving the targets. Business Plan Deployment brings these aspects together with the dimensions of coordination and consistent reviews for all 5 aspects of business performance including; Safety, Quality, Cost, Delivery and HR development.

The planning process starts with top management setting the goals of the organisation, then passing them down to the next level for the determining of objectives to achieve them. When the goals and objectives have been agreed, the unit management level establishes with their superiors the performance targets to be set. The targets are then broken down to group leader and team level, such that the targets can be confirmed as achievable, and outline plans developed to say how they can be achieved.

The 5 aspects are used across every department so every one is focused on improving these key performance indicators for the company.

During the target setting phase, it is the task of the shop floor to come up with outline plans/activities that they believe will achieve the targets. In doing so they are confirming that the targets agreed are not just a wish list.

These outline plans will be fed up the organisation and the targets and plans may go back and forth a number of times before being agreed as a practical business plan. However by doing this the workforce becomes very familiar with the challenge and is confident because it is more than a wish list.

Quite often a "stretch" target is set to create some challenge over and above the current thinking, and quality circle groups are established to find ways to achieve these elevated targets.

Fig. 3

Tracking of the Business Plan is carried out continuously using the PDCA management cycle (Plan, Do, Check, Action).

Below is shown a typical BPD information board using the PDCA format for easier tracking. As can be seen on this board the complete plan and targets are shown for each of the 5 aspects and month by month progress is recorded on the performance charts.

Regular reviews are carried out at this board by management to understand any problems and to give support where necessary.

Later in the book we will talk more about the PDCA management cycle and how it can be used to ensure activities stay on course while at the same time being used to encourage and give timely support to the workforce.

Fig. 4

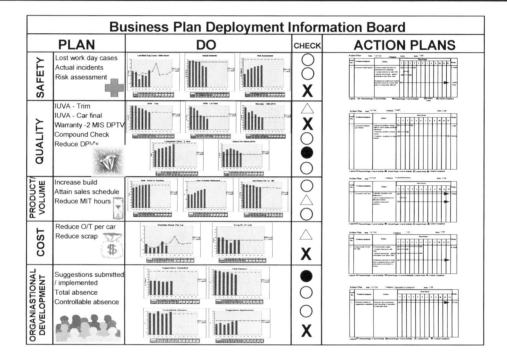

Where an item does not achieve its monthly target the check box will be marked with an **X** indicating that an action plan is required. The action plan must be identified immediately.

If the shortfall to target is minimal and will be achieved without special action a **triangle** will be placed in the check box.

If the target is achieved the check box will be marked with **O**.

This activity requires involvement from the workforce and in part III. I will identify ways in which this can be achieved.

It must be clearly understood that to keep the vision practical, having a methodology to achieve it and a process to track progress is of paramount importance to becoming lean, as without them, progress will slip back without being noticed.

Actions

Review whether your company has a vision. If the answer is no you can follow these steps to develop one:

- Determine your current performance versus your planning base and fully understand the gaps.

- Determine your current competitiveness versus your competition or alternatively, if you supply to a 1st tier customer, what will make you their supplier of choice.

- Identify what activities will be required to achieve the desired outcome and a sensible time frame to get there, if your knowledge is low on lean manufacturing use one of the many consulting groups to audit your plant to establish which activities will suit your needs. Remember you do not have to use the support activities of the consultant.

- Seek ways of improving your management teams understanding of lean manufacturing.

- Consider employing a manager who has good knowledge of lean manufacturing, but be very conscious of changes he will want to implement, so make him your partner as the architect of the vision.

- Develop a plan to deploy the vision to the total work force. Use diagonal slice meetings* to discuss what it means to your employees, what will be expected of them, how they will be supported and any concerns that may arise.

- Establish these improvement activities as the basis for your annual Business Plan. Share the targets at shop floor management level and encourage them to develop activities with their team leaders.

- Implement a tracking system to identify progress, good or bad, and use it as a basis for improving the planning activity.

Vision and Business Plan

Diagonal slice: to bring people together from various levels and departments to give feedback, discuss and plan actions to overcome a company wide issue.

Creating mutual benefits for all stakeholders

World Class Organisations are able to track all cost savings activities to measure their true impact on the bottom line performance of the Company, they have a system for relating this in terms of the following year's requirements to investment, share holder return and monetary recognition for a successful year.

They therefore create a transparent system for determining how the savings will be shared with the workforce in a way that matches potential monetary benefits with required performance targets.

This has replaced the annual wage negotiation with an activity of consensus decision making using criteria such as: level of savings achieved, investment money needed for the coming year, and wage increases being applied by competitors within the industry. For example, sometimes if investment requirements are high during the next year, it may be decided to improve other areas of the benefits package which spread the costs more beneficially.

The point that these companies focus on is that the employees must see that the company is open and honest about performance and is transparent about how savings are shared.

It is important that when considering the *overall benefits package*, the workforce say "this is a good company to work for".

Too often the traditional annual wage negotiation gives the impression that the company wants to take all of the hard earned savings for themselves and the trade unions have to fight tooth and nail for any increase. How therefore do you think the people are going to feel about working for the company while under this impression?

If you are to succeed in developing a world class performance from your organisation it is necessary for you to determine how you will ensure there are mutual benefits for all of your workforce as well as the company and its customers. The benefits will not all be equal but the savings have to be distributed in a way that is seen to be fair to all stakeholders.

The customer should benefit from receiving high quality products, competitively priced, as and when they want them.

For the company it is important that money is generated for investment into the business for future viability, plus enough to provide a decent return on investment for its shareholders, which is above the rate they can receive from placing their money in a bank.

Finally the workforce needs to feel it is being compensated for the effort they put into producing the products for sale by the company.

This should not be just about money, it is important to consider the total benefits package that you can make available including sickness and accident benefit, family health care plan, employee discounts on the products you produce. If you produce parts that go into larger products discuss with the end producer whether discounts can be given to your employees. Also such items as crèche or child care activities from local support organisations that can provide a service should be considered.

Then on the money side, it is important that your employees can support their families and are not constantly in fear of losing everything (Maslow's "hierarchy of needs" - see Fig. 16, p. 80). Salary compensation needs to be competitive within the industry, but must be viewed in terms of the total benefit package, and the annual increase should be considered against a targeted cost reduction/ profit picture established at the beginning of the year so everyone knows what the targets are and the potential benefits of attaining them.

Within your strategy you should consider being able to ensure your workforce pay increase at least meets the cost of living index, such that they will not fall behind the cost of living.

Based on performance there should be a methodology to determine how much of the savings should go into base pay increase (enough to stay competitive in salaries), with the rest going into a one time bonus payment, reflecting in total the workforce share of the cost savings.

Another very important subject to cover is job security and production capacity, and how you intend to react to customer demand (increase and decrease) particularly with reference to the size of the company workforce. The vision needs to build the confidence of the core workforce that their jobs are as safe as anybody could make them and that during normal operating conditions their annual salary increase will never lag behind the cost of living index.

The way that world class manufacturers do this is by utilising a two step strategy to manage volatility of demand.

In step 1 they employ approximately 10% of the workforce as temporary or agency labour to help absorb slight fluctuations to normal customer demand.

As demand increases, step 2, mandatory overtime, is used to meet the rising demand.

Up to 2hours overtime per shift can be called in 15 minute increments to provide the additional units for each shift/day. The company expectations are shared in the quarterly "Health of the Company" report-back to the workforce so they know what level of planned overtime to expect. This is then confirmed month by month.

This overtime can also be called for shifts where the originally planned output was not met for any reason, and notice is given to those affected by the third break of the day, to allow people to phone home to warn their partners. This is based on JIT principles that product should be produced when it is required in the quantities required according to customer demand. Therefore the shift build requirements must be met. Needless to say the workforce works on plans to reduce the occurrences of missed output and therefore the amount of overtime called.

Saturday and Sunday overtime can also be called for additional production requirements. Advanced warning is normally given of the potential dates at the beginning of the year so the workforce can plan accordingly and confirmation is given two months prior to the actual dates.

This weekend overtime is not used for catch-up of lost production. Under the concept of Just in Time production this must happen immediately when the short fall is caused.

When customer demand falls, first the overtime is stopped, and then if a greater reduction is required, the temporary/agency workers will be laid off.

Temporary/agency workers can achieve core employee status through attrition in the core workforce; the temporary/agency person is then replaced by hiring from outside the company.

In this way job security is promised to all core employees for their support in applying the two steps and this is written into the terms and conditions of employment.

Although the workforce is generally satisfied by the agreement and understands that the overtime call is a way of protecting their jobs, management has to use common sense that if the customer demand is going to stay high for a considerable amount of time, weekend overtime will not be sustainable due to the commitments of employees to their families.

Consideration must be given to alternative ways of increasing the output thus reducing the weekend overtime. Kaizen activities are applied to the processes to reduce waste and increase value added work output, but if necessary the workforce will be increased.

The important point to note is that everyone benefits from the improvement activities, the company through reduced overtime costs and the workforce by reduced encroachment on family time and stable employment.

Mutual Benefits

Actions

- Review your monetary reward system to see if its rewards are based on bottom line performance impact or just for participation.

- Establish with your Financial and Human Resources Development experts a proper reward system as close as possible to that described above and determine a plan to discuss with Trade Unions and the workforce.

- Consider a trial period (up to 3 years) to see how it works and to make improvements that can be observed before establishing it as a permanent process. Considerable training and follow will be required to establish a positive consensus decision making activity with your Trade Unions and management team

- Ensure that the requirements for daily continuous improvement activities, overtime etc. are included in the terms of contracts of all employees.

Beliefs, Values & their supporting Behaviours

To achieve the kind of performance tracking and problem solving needed is a big challenge for the vast majority of Companies. If you want to stand any chance of sustainability you will have to ensure the total involvement and support of your workforce.

To get everyone on board will need changes mentioned earlier in your production system and in your compensation system. But just as important is the way that everyone behaves from Managing Director down to the operator on the shop floor.

This will almost certainly require a change in the way people in your company behave. This can best be understood by listing the actual behaviours/practices predominant in the company and trying to align them with any stated Beliefs & Values held by officers of the company.

It is no good asking for trust and full participation if people perceive managers to be dishonest and disrespectful to them. On the other hand managers trying to manage a workforce that continuously cuts corners and lets poor quality workmanship go is not acceptable either.

All companies operate within a collection of beliefs and values even if they have never been written down; they are visible through the behaviours of its management team and its workforce!

Examples of unofficial beliefs:

The workforce never puts in the necessary effort to reduce costs. (management).

No one cares what I think so I only come here for the money. (workforce).

These are two typical examples made *visible* by management placing considerable pressure on the workforce to work faster with overburdened operations, and the corresponding workforce behaviour of indifference, voicing the opinion "so what if it goes wrong as long as I am paid at the end of the month"?

Both beliefs create negative behaviours that result in considerable resistance to performance improvement, which inhibits cost reduction and actually prevents maximising of profits.

To ensure that the organisation works together and focuses on supporting the key players for the success of the company, a mutually binding set of beliefs and values must be established. But beliefs and values are not enough, there has to be a set of behaviours identified and practiced to ensure the beliefs and values are demonstrated in the daily business of the company.

These behaviours should concentrate thinking, on how the total organisation bonds into a cohesive working unit, that trusts each of the various elements to work for the good of the company and its workforce.

Mans first set of Beliefs and Values

Having a set of beliefs and values that ensures that the company and its workforce benefits from successful improvement activities is key to winning the total support of all stakeholders.

Openness and honesty are the bedrocks for setting up beliefs and values that are believed and universally applied by all members of the organisation.

Tough subjects such as more efficient working practices and headcount reduction, can only be worked out face to face with the work force, in a frank and honest manner, whilst respecting the dignity of those that might be affected.

Concerns must be addressed and managed speedily in an understanding manner, to limit stress and tension in the work force. This can only be done, if there is a frame work of the company's stated beliefs and values to apply, when dealing with working relationships.

In a world class manufacturing organisation beliefs and values start with recognising who it is that directly generates revenue for the company.

They are the people who provide the products or services that are sold by the company.

They are also the people responsible for producing the product at as low a cost as possible.

All other departments recognise that they exist to support the production department reach their quality, output, cost, safety and development targets. It has to be recognised that on a day to day basis the most important thing in the company is the generation of revenue.

For example an engineer who is too busy to immediately go and support a manufacturing problem is operating to the wrong set of beliefs and values and no matter how important he might say production is, his behaviour gives him away.

Over the long term the project he is working on may be important to the company, but if revenue generation stops, the project may not be necessary.

Successful companies are very clear about their beliefs and values and go as far as describing the behaviours that must be visible. These are integrated into the performance assessments of the workforce and 360 degree* feedback is given to all management people.

In addition to this an employee opinion survey is carried out every 18 months on how well the management team is managing the business with particular reference to their management behaviours.

From this feedback actions are determined to improve the management process in line with the critique received.

*360 degree assessments means feedback is given from your boss, your peers and your subordinates with reference to the degree you display the required behaviours against scoring criteria.

Beliefs and Values should not be a wishy-washy set of principles that just look good, but each belief and value must support an important need of the company;

Addressing the need to continuously reduce costs and generate revenue for the security of the company and its workforce.

The need to fully involve the workforce in all decisions related to their processes.

Supporting the need to develop a relationship based on mutual trust between management and the workforce.

The need to get consensus on all decisions (instead of management decisions shoehorned in against significant opposition or apathy).

The need to let the people with the knowledge make decisions based on clearly drafted business needs criteria. The following are examples of business needs criteria:

The decision must impact favourably the cost structure of the business.

The decision must be in alignment with the company (Just in Time) production principles.

There must not be any adverse impact on the health & safety of employees or the quality of the product they produce.

The decision must not contradict the beliefs and values of the company.

These criteria are applied using proper performance data to allow measurement of objective achievement.

Working to these criteria there is no reason why decisions can not be made at operator level generating higher levels of job satisfaction.

Detailed below are some typical beliefs and values from leading world class companies which are used to guide their behaviours and practices:

The needs of the company support the needs of our people.

For the long term stability/development of the business it is important that the company and its employees satisfy their needs. There must be mutual benefit in all that is undertaken.

The company must make sufficient profit to satisfy shareholders and invest in new equipment/products for the future, whilst at the same time endeavour to maintain the ability of the individual to support his/her family by sharing the results of cost reduction activities in an equitable manner.

The employees on the other hand must understand the two parts of their employment agreement, first to carry out their primary job function as described and secondly to participate in daily improvement of all activities.

Behaviour:

The Company has an agreed remuneration system with the Trade Union/ workforce that is based on consensus not negotiation and which takes into consideration: investments needed for the coming years, company cost savings levels achieved, and industry norms in terms of benefit packages. The employees are fully engaged in improvement activities as well as their primary job function.

There is always open, honest and sincere communication

Communication on the state of the business is carried out directly from top management and face to face if possible.

In larger organisations it is understood this may not be possible, so video format should be considered to ensure all people get the same message directly from top management.

A system for feedback will be set up so that the communication is always two ways with a positive reception given to all concerns.

The answers to all concerns will be given back as swiftly as possible. When members do not understand a decision, time will be taken to explain it in the frame work of the needs of the business criteria mentioned earlier.

The communication no matter how difficult will be carried out honestly and with empathy.

Behaviour:

The Company keeps the workforce fully informed on the state of the business every quarter and has diagonal slice and lunch box meetings to discuss concerns and ideas for resolving them. A concerns tracking system is put in place to resolve all concerns.

Living by the concept of challenge.

It is important that a long term vision is shared and understood by the workforce and that the associated challenges are clearly spelt out such that they can be tackled with courage and creativity to realise the vision.

The challenges should be about creating value through the manufacturing and delivery of products and services.

Encouraging the spirit of challenge will be done in such a way that the organisation will willingly take on stretch targets for performance with no blame attached if the stretch is not quite achieved.

We will always consider the long term impact as well as the short term gain to ensure decisions do not negatively impact our future.

Thorough consideration in decision making will be applied to ensure decisions are measured against appropriate criteria and that all view points are listened to and considered.

Behaviour:

Management encourages the workforce to take on stretch targets, positively looking for ways to support their efforts to achieve them. Management celebrate not only success but good efforts also and do not blame people if the stretch target is not quite achieved.

Shop Floor focus.

"We practice going to the work place, going to the source to find the facts to make correct decisions, build consensus and achieve goals at our best speed."

This helps to build effective consensus building, by going to see the facts and discuss with the people directly involved what is happening.

Management going to the shop floor builds commitment to achievement by everyone when they see how important their daily activity is to the success of the company.

Everybody in the organisation understands that revenue is generated by the shop floor activity therefore supporting it must take priority over everything else.

Behaviour:

Management regularly attend concerns and performance reviews on the shop floor. They demonstrate interest and commitment to assist teams that are struggling with problems. They celebrate success with teams that are achieving improvements. (see chapter 9 for a world class review method)

Management discuss issues on the shop floor sooner than in the office, therefore giving first hand advice and support to the workforce.

Continuous Improvement in all we do.

"We improve our business operations continuously, always driving for innovation and evolution."

Develop a kaizen mind and innovative thinking within the workforce, by teaching new skills and encouraging daily participation in improvement activities.

Build Lean Systems and Structures to ensure cost effective performance.

Promote organisational learning by learning from every thing that happens, positive and negative, and by encouraging the adoption of new practices and skills wherever possible.

Behaviour:

Using all problems and target shortfalls as opportunities to improve and learn from. The manager encourages teams to take on performance issues and countermeasure them such that daily improvement becomes the norm.

Never looking for whom to blame but looking at what-why-when and who can help resolve the issue!!

Respect

"We respect others, make every effort to understand each other, take responsibility and do our best to build mutual trust."

Respect stakeholders by involving them in decisions that affect their workplace, supplying practical criteria which enables them to participate in consensus decision making.

To give mutual trust and take mutual responsibility by allowing decisions to be taken where they are needed.

Promoting sincere communication such that difficult subjects can be addressed openly and trust is developed in the solutions.

Behaviour:

The management team sets up a process that enables the workforce to make decisions on all items affecting their workplace and the workforce responds by making decisions based on established criteria in a responsible manner.

Management provides opportunities for the workforce to communicate their opinions and ideas about company objectives/activities, they respond to the ideas in a positive manner looking for ways to use the good ideas.

Teamwork

"We stimulate personal and professional growth, share the opportunities of development and maximise individual and team performance."

Commit positively to the education and development of employees to enable them to discover their full potential.

Show respect for the individual while realising consolidated power as a team, by ensuring that they have input into everything that affects their team performance.

Behaviour:

Management demonstrate good interdepartmental teamwork in all they do, sharing resources and always supporting one another. They promote and support team working activities such as 5S, improvement teams, back up teams and quality circles, acting as mentors to the team leaders.

I stress again that Beliefs and Values are not just statements that hang on the Managing Directors office wall to show visitors. They must be shared with every member of the organisation and must have detailed behaviours and practices that turn them into a reality.

As mentioned above performance appraisal systems should be used to feedback on the application of the beliefs and values, using a 360 degree format, giving the opportunity for direct reports, peers and supervisors to give feedback from their perspective.

In reviewing this feedback the manager looks to align the results from all levels by adjusting his/her behaviour. Good feedback from the boss while getting negative feedback from direct reports can indicate a too task focussed person who drives sooner than leads.

Much damage is done when beliefs and values are rolled out as the latest project to "involve people" when there are no supporting behaviours and practices put in place.

Employees consider it to be insincere and just a trick to make management appear progressive while nothing really changes.

Management are inevitably disappointed when the workforce does not respond positively, little realising that they themselves behaved in the same old manner which incites the same old responses.

Having the correct set of Beliefs and Values and exhibiting behaviour aligned to them, is very important if you wish to introduce the "Concept of Challenge" as described in the next chapter, as you must overcome the fear of failure.

Later in this book you can read about ways to empower your workforce, demonstrating trust in their knowledge and abilities and strengthening the Beliefs and Values of the Company.

Diagonal slice: to bring people together from various levels and departments to give feedback, discuss and plan actions to overcome a company wide issue.

Beliefs

Values

Actions

- Determine what the beliefs and values of your organisation really are, take steps to ensure they are practical and avoid the clichés.

- Define the behaviours and practices that will support the beliefs and values.

- Ask your employees to give feedback in a behaviour survey, to tell you how far away your behaviours and practices are, from where you need them to be to support your beliefs and values.

- Plan and prioritise actions to bring you in line with your beliefs and values. Involve all levels of the organisation thus creating an environment of believable change.

- Change the mind set of employees who have a poor perception of management by involving them in diagonal slice meetings* and action groups to bring about the improvement.

- Consider introducing a 360 degree performance assessment review process for each manager so that he receives feedback from all levels of the organisation on his behaviour.

2. The Lean Organisation

Conventional vs Lean organisations

There is much discussion about organisations that are flat, versus those with a more hierarchical number of levels and even matrix type organisations. Sometimes companies plan management positions with the focus on maximising span of control, even if it means combining departments that do not belong together.

One organisation I know of had combined the HR manager and Quality manager function under one person! Unfortunately he did not have the time to carry out both functions.

The focus when developing an organisation structure, is that it should reflect the way you want to run your business, because the structure will re-enforce behaviours that are aligned to it.

That is to say, if the organisation is hierarchical, the practices within the company will tend to be bureaucratic and will not encourage decisions to be taken at the working level. The overall perception being that "he is the manager" and is therefore paid to make decisions.

To illustrate this point we will review the two structures shown in Fig. 5 and Fig. 6. These are two examples taken from the Auto industry. The first is a conventional mass production organisation while the second is a typical lean organisation.

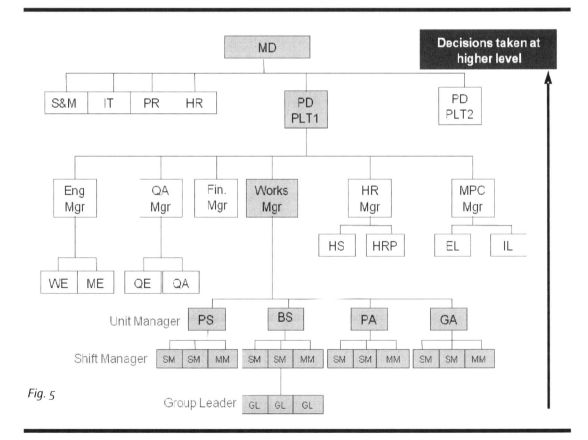

Fig. 5

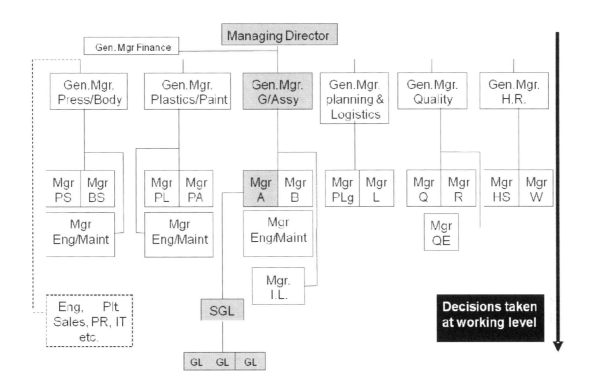

Fig. 6

Key

S&M - Sales & Marketing
IT – Information Technology
PR – Public Relations
HR – Human Resources management
PD – Plant Director
Eng – Engineering
QA – Quality Assurance
HS – Health & Safety
HRP – Human resources planning
EL – External logistics
FIN—Finance
IL – Internal logistics
MPC—Material Production Control

WE – Works engineering
ME – Manufacturing engineering
MM—Maintenance Manager
QE – Quality engineering
PS – Press shop
BS- Body shop
PA – Paint shop
GA – General assembly
PL – Plastics shop
PLg – Planning
L – Logistics
Q – Quality
R- Reliability
W—Welfare
SGL—Senior Group Leader

It can be seen that although the lean organisation has less levels, it does in fact have more headcount from M.D. level down to unit manager. So the decision of using a flat structure is not solely about span of control, but more about putting support and expertise where it is needed.

The question is not simply which is the better organisation structure; to be flatter or have more levels and fewer managers with greater span of control, but what are the drivers for your business.

Higher levels of diverse technical input **may** call for a more hierarchical structure while employing other means of involving the workforce, who may not be technically skilled.

However in companies where the level of revenue generated is clearly driven by the abilities and commitment of the workforce, a flatter more team working orientated structure would be preferable.

Clearly the answer lies in how you want to structure and run your business, either with hierarchical managers making decisions and taking responsibility or with the workforce taking the decisions and the responsibility for their actions.

But for organisations who require managers to manage (not lead), that is to say make decisions and ensure everyone complies with them, then clearly organisation shown in Fig. 5 is the only option.

This type of organisation is most often found in companies that do not have good levels of understanding of the business needs throughout the organisation. In most of these organisations there is no perceived mutual benefit attainable from company activities.

Because of this there is a tendency towards a conflictual relationship between management and the workforce representatives.

Therefore initiatives tend to be management driven and workers only come to work to do clearly defined manual tasks.

What one finds typically in this type of organisation is that not only is the manager fighting the workforce to get decisions implemented, but also half of the management team who have their own priorities.

The organisation in Fig.5 actually drives decisions upwards in the organisation because there are people there to do it i.e. the works manager responsible for all of the manufacturing units and the Plant Director who has responsibility for everything in the plant. After all that's why they are there, isn't it!

On one occasion during a visit to an assembly plant, I was walking with the works manager through the assembly shop, when he suddenly stopped and berated an operator who was reading an article in a news paper.

"I am paid to watch you work not to watch you read the news paper" he shouted at the top of his voice, needless to say the operator was extremely embarrassed.

It was an eye opener to find out what a works manager gets paid for, but even more ironic, was that the article being read was about the potential difficulties the plant was going to face in the near future, something which had not been shared with the workforce in the plant!

This was a clear case of Fig. 5 logic, managers are there to manage people and the workforce is there to do as they are told.

However, beware! Decisions made in a Plant Directors conference room, no matter how well meant, are not always practical and quite often not supported by the workforce.

This inevitably leads to delays and poor start up when teething problems are experienced, due to the workforce taking a "told you so" position, standing back and letting maintenance and the engineers contain the issue and provide a countermeasure!.

It should also be noted that in this type of organisation, politics tend to take over from good common sense decision making, thus making the various levels less effective in the way they work together.

If you want your people to become committed to the future of the company, they will need to become stakeholders in all aspects of the work they perform. They will need to be able to make decisions on health & safety, quality, output, cost and even development requirements. For this type of operating organisation shown in Fig. 6 clearly is the best option.

In Fig. 6 there is no Plant Director or Works manager the general managers of the business report directly to the Managing Director and the unit managers report directly to them.

This makes it imperative that the General Managers are very strategic and think as a group for the good of the company, they can not afford to have disagreements that need reference upwards. The Managing Director's scope of responsibility does not allow him to be the day to day operations decision maker.

In this organisation the general managers have to be the best team in the plant and their behaviour has to encourage the pushing down of decisions to where the decision is needed.

They ensure that skills and resources are shared across the plant when the need arises. They ensure that unit managers work together on development of solutions to problems or challenges.

In short the general managers become leaders, guides and coaches of the workforce from unit manager down to team member.

They ensure that business knowledge is shared and used together with member skills,

so that decisions on performance improvement are practical and in line with business needs.

Because decisions are not made in isolation and are made at the working level, everyone supports and ensures that they are successful.

To ensure that the decisions are accepted, it is imperative that team working and consensus decision making are the focus from this organisation.

Lean business unit structure

The Fig. 6 organisation creates a matrix approach to managing certain aspects of the business e.g. finance. The manager must take full responsibility for the financial performance of his unit. However the Financial Director must have overall control of company finances, thus will assign a member of the finance department as a support member to the manager.

The other difference that can be seen is the level of responsibility that the general manager takes for his units; he is responsible for everything including engineering, finance, internal logistics, health & safety, human resources management and development.

Fig 7 shows a lean responsibility structure for a production department and it can be seen that typically Finance, H&S, and HR are picked up by the production manager but has support people assigned to him from the originating departments.

BUSINESS UNIT STRUCTURE

It can be seen that some departments play a supporting role to production whilst at the same time playing a leading role in establishing policy, or legislative guidelines.

In a lean organisation, members from these departments have functional dotted lines to the production general manager .
They support him in establishing realistic budgets (Finance), in applying HR policies and ensuring H&S legislation is understood and properly adopted (HR).

Process engineering, maintenance and internal materials management all come under the responsibility of the production general manager as shown in the figure. This is to ensure that joint decisions are made between supporting departments and the production team, that are focussed on the needs of the business, the company production principles and the beliefs and values of the organisation.

The company support activities such as QA, engineering services and production planning/external logistics are carried out in a more traditional manner, although team building and consensus decision making is a strong feature in ensuring decisions are made for the good of the business.

In the mass production model, all of these activities are run independently in silo type organisations, creating sub optimisation and relying on the Plant Director to intervene when agreement is not reached.

One of the key aspects of involving the workforce is to ensure responsibility is placed with the people who have to live with the decisions, that is to say: the people who must make it work. It is important that they take ownership of any projects or activities that directly affects their ability to perform their work function. This means they have to take a leading role co-ordinating the various activities; technical, logistic, training, risk assessments etc. It does not mean they have to have technical skills; the planning engi-

neers retain the responsibility to ensure all technical details are safe and practical. But the production department must take overall responsibility for successful implementation and start up.

During my years with General Motors I experienced the impact of working in both manners and observed the different reactions of the same team members to the situation.

Prior to the formation of the joint venture between Bedford Commercial Vehicles (GM) and Isuzu Motors, projects were run by engineers with the support of maintenance and production was kept informed of what was going to happen.

The communication of progress was normally quite good but the involvement of production was absolutely nominal until production start up, then production was expected to take over.

However when teething problems were experienced, the production members stopped production and waited for engineering and maintenance to sort the problem out before continuing. This often resulted in delays and considerable frustration for all parties.

After the formation of the joint venture, all projects/changes were directed through the production organisation, this gave them more input into what was going to happen, as well as the responsibility for co-ordination and production start up.

The change in the people was phenomenal. Issues were discussed and resolved during the early stages of the activity, and if teething problems were experienced, the production team provided containment while the issue was resolved. The same people, who six months earlier reacted negatively to these issues, now were the most positive members of the project team and nothing was going to stop start up.

Actions

- Investigate your organisational structure. Are decisions driven up the organisation to Managers who are removed from where the action happens?

- If the structure drives the wrong way, determine what can be done to reverse the direction and drive the decision back down the organisation to where the action is needed?

- Determine how you can make your Unit Management responsible for all decisions applicable for the unit? E.g. if engineering reports elsewhere how can you ensure that all changes must be brought off by all levels of unit management?

The Lean Organisation

3. Consensus Decision Making

Because decisions are not hierarchical in lean organisations, consensus plays a very big part in the success of its activities so it is important that we take a little time to understand how this works.

Definition of "consensus decision making".

"Genuine consensus typically requires more focus on developing the relationships among stakeholders, so that they work together to achieve agreements based on willing consent.

Consensus usually involves collaboration, rather than compromise. Instead of one opinion being adopted by the group, stakeholders are brought together (often with facilitation) until a convergent decision is developed.

Consensus normally is easier to achieve if criteria is used to test potential solutions against".

To enable decisions to be pushed down to shop floor level into the remit of the Team Leader and team Members, there has to be a process for ensuring good business decisions are made.

Decision Making Criteria

With so many stakeholders in the decision making process, it is important to get consensus and this can only be done effectively if decision making criteria is used.
These criteria should always ensure that the action is :

- In line with the needs of the business,

- Supports the Production System principles.

- Aligned with the beliefs and values of the organisation.

The group leader facilitating a consensus decision should ensure that measurable results of the change support these 3 criteria.

If there is a negative result against one of the criteria he should look for modification to come into compliance.

Example of criteria:

Criteria 1 Needs of the business:

Defined as achieving improvement in customer received quality and/or mandatory cost reductions to meet pricing targets. (measured in PPM defects and financial bottom line cost reduction)

Current first time quality performance must be improved if possible but must not be compromised. (Current Defects per Product compared to Defects per Product after change)

No negative impact on quality/reduced risk. If possible, a form of error proofing or successive inspection should be added to the process to ensure changes do not add to the risk of a defect being caused.

The process steps must be scrutinised to ensure that they have not created hard to control assembly conditions that could result in a defect being created. If such a risk is discovered the team must redesign the process to remove it.

Cost must be reduced by eliminating waste and simplifying processes. (financial cost reduction)

Labour, scrap & rework, indirect materials and energy consumption must not be increased; they should be reduced if possible. (financial cost reduction in each account)

Criteria 2 Production System Principles:

Must follow the defined lean principles e.g. Just in time production process flow with all waste eliminated. (No buffers introduced, lean principles applied)

Criteria 3 Alignment with beliefs and values:

Solutions should comply with the company's Beliefs & Values.

For example reducing overhead costs by changing equipment should not burden an operator with over cycle processes or ergonomic issues.

It is very important to make the actual criteria as measurable as possible so that everyone can see the improvement the decision will provide.

Decision making Process

Using criteria should mean that no department or person can push a bad decision or stand in the way of a good decision. It is the group leader's responsibility to ensure all ideas are considered and that everyone affected has input.

Normally the department which is intending to make a change will announce its plans to the local unit management; the group leader will ensure that all relevant parties have been invited to the meeting. This will include other departments, e.g. internal logistics, as well as team leaders and members who work on the process affected.

The plans will be discussed in detail and time will be given for all parties to review the impact of the planned change and report back at a follow up meeting. The engineering group and the production group are required to confirm the likelihood of achieving the criteria. The group leader, supported by his unit manager, will act as the meeting leader if the impact of the change affects production.

Any concerns will be worked through until a consensus decision can be made based on the agreed criteria. Should there be a dead-lock between departments, the managers of the departments will be invited to the next full meeting to help remove the roadblock. Where the concern is not criteria related, agreement should be made about how to handle the concern through tracking/action, to reduce as much as possible a perceived negative impact on a person or group.

This can slow down the decision making process but experience shows that when a decision is made it has full support and progresses very quickly to fruition.

On completion of the change, one week's worth of production activity is followed to ensure performance is where it was expected to be.

In conventional organisations decisions are taken quickly by management only to be frustrated during implementation because there has been no consensus and therefore no buy in.

This is easily observed when an improve-ment is being proposed by one shift and the other reacts with the "not invented here" syndrome. Arguments continue for weeks and months to get the change in and quite often wasteful compromises are made.

It is well known that Japanese companies take more time consulting with all stake-holders before making important strategic decisions, then implement very quickly.

I experienced this first hand at Toyota and it was very impressive if not a little scary, to witness the speed in which implementation took place and the level of support from all areas and levels of the organisation.

Actions

Review your decision making process:

- Educate you total organisation on the criteria to be used for decision making ensuring that they are aware the decision must be made by the people affected by the ac-tivity.

- Make your first line supervisors responsible for ensuring criteria have been defined for decision making and shop floor workers are consulted and reach consensus for all decisions affecting their work processes.

- Set up a management review of shop floor decisions, reviewing the decision making process as well as the decision itself.

- Ensure the management team use the reviews to coach consensus and actively support when the de-cision making is stalled.

4. Shop Floor Focus

The concept of "Shop Floor Focus" is to put focus where the company revenue is generated and ensure that nothing inhibits the potential for ever increasing revenue.

Every department including Finance, HR, Engineering, Logistics, Quality Assurance and Maintenance, etc. must ensure that the production department gets all of the support needed to not only manufacture the product, but also to improve the cost effectiveness of their operations.

Members must be empowered to decide what needs to be done to achieve a particular goal and support must be available to help them carry out the required action e.g. engineering or maintenance, etc.

This means that there must be effective ways of tracking performance and the concerns that get raised when trying to reach a performance improvement target.

Visual Management of the workplace

Visual management must be used to keep members and management informed of current progress so that timely action can be taken to prevent revenue loss, it should also track and indicate whether countermeasures are succeeding.

Visual management tools must be used in the workplace to indicate the status of production activities, in such a way that even a stranger entering the workshop would see the key performance indicators and understand which activities require supporting.

Key performance indicators need to indicate both daily performance and long term improvement activity progress.

For daily performance management, key performance indicators predominantly show ; member difficulty (Andon), Quality, equipment downtime, material delivery status and build performance data, so that actions can be taken immediately a problem arises that might prevent the shift targets being attained. The visual management tools should include audio/visual indicators for quick response.

For long term improvement activities, the key performance indicators display performance against BPD plan in the 5 aspects : H&S, Quality, Delivery, Cost and Human resources development. This will be visible for all to see and to react to.

Concerns Management & Escalation

Most manufacturing systems, because they are complex and dynamic, generate many concerns that can prevent the workforce performing to the best of their ability. Therefore it is very important to have a process with which to manage the problem solving and counter measuring of these concerns.

This means that the concerns resolution process must be a vigorous visual management communication tool clearly indicating who is responsible for resolving the concern.

Every concern should first be tackled by the people it affects most, so the working team should make the first attempt to resolve it.

When the concern clearly can not be resolved by the team, the concern should be put onto the group leaders concern tracking list which is placed in a prominent place in the workshop.

The concerns tracking list shown in chart 8 (parts A & B) identifies the following information :

- Concern item number given by the supervisor when adding to the list.

- The date the concern was added to the list.

- The Team number of the team raising the concern

- The process number affected.

- A ranking is given based on level of affect on team performance.

- The name of the team member who raised the concern (only this person can ok the concern countermeasure)

- Description of concern

Fig. 8—Part A

	ITEM N°	Date	Team N°	# N°	Rank	Member	Concern
Concerns Tracking List							

Rank Key:

A= Potential safety concern or concern cannot be or is difficult to contain

B= no affect to safety and can be contained with support

C= no affect to group kpi or members and does not require support.

Name of Group Leader :

_____

kpi = key performance indicator

- Details of investigation

- Details of countermeasure

- Name of person responsible for solution

- Target completion date

- Actual completion date

- Status of countermeasure

This sheet is used for identifying all concerns in progress and is supported by a progress tracking sheet (Fig. 9 next page). The progress tracking sheet is used to ensure proper escalation of the concern if countermeasures are too slow.

Fig. 8—Part B

Investigation	Countermeasure	Responsible	Tgt. Date	Act.Date	Conf.

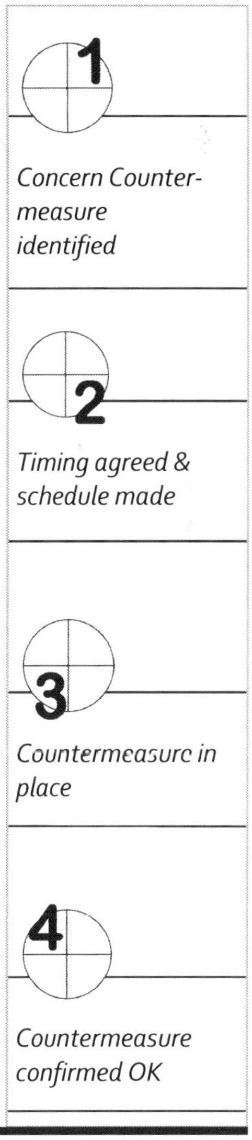

1 — Concern Countermeasure identified

2 — Timing agreed & schedule made

3 — Countermeasure in place

4 — Countermeasure confirmed OK

Concerns Progress Sheet

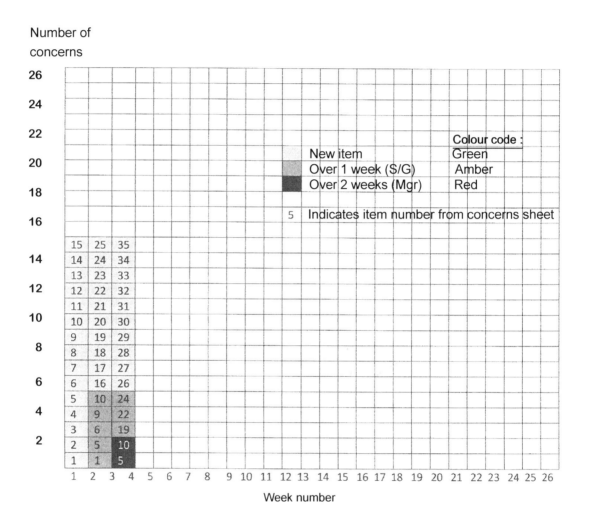

Fig. 9

The group leader takes over the responsibility for ensuring action is taken to resolve the issue, calling together support groups and responsible engineers to help. (Green colour code)

Each concern is reviewed at a weekly meeting chaired by the group leader, at which all supporting groups report on progress to resolve the concerns. This meeting is always held in the workplace so on the spot clarification can be carried out.

If the concern is not resolved within the following week the senior group leader becomes involved in the activity, supporting the group leader with other departments to accelerate the problem solving activity and driving to resolution. (Amber colour code)

If after a further week the solution has not been identified, the unit manager must become involved in removing any roadblocks and obtaining necessary support from departmental managers. (Red colour code) He is obliged to report the concern after one more week to the general manager group who will coordinate support activities across the organisation. This very rarely occurs, normally only for items that need input from a source external to the plant i.e. engineering change, or changes to supplier tooling.

The visual management system for the escalation is posted on the group leader's board and each week the colour coding is altered to show where the concern is in the process.

The colour coding identifies which stage of follow the concern is in, making it very easy for the unit manager to step in at the right moment.

It also allows higher management to see when a concern is not being resolved, so that immediate steps can be taken to remove the road block to progress.

This is a very powerful tool which, particularly when the group leader is overstretched, ensures that a supporting activity is introduced via the escalation process. No concern waits for the group leader to find the time to progress it!

Needless to say management must ensure that the concern resolution process is managed correctly and not allowed to fall behind. It demonstrates a strong commitment from management and shows how seriously they take work place concerns.

Too many weeks of red activity demonstrates poor commitment from management displayed for all to see!!

Under no circumstances must the shop floor team be left, feeling that they are pushing problems up hill. They must get immediate responses to concerns they can not resolve themselves and must be informed about when a solution will be available.

Shop Floor Performance Reviews

All performance reviews should be held on the shop floor using the various visual management information boards available (shown below). There should be no need for written reports for anything other than the daily output performance. In this case the written report is used to inform the opposite shift and other departments of performance difficulties and actions taken.

Of course data must be collected for inclusion in company reports, for reporting to higher management or to a mother plant which may be situated in a different location. But the point is that shop floor personnel should not be bogged down sending reports to management. Rather management should be reviewing the abundance of visual information on the shop floor.

Many companies copying lean make the mistake of requiring written versions of the information boards and hold conference room meetings to discuss issues arising from them.

These are not shop floor focused companies they are still conference room focused. They also double the work for production department creating non value added waste.

The advantage of shop floor reviews is that conditions/concerns etc. can immediately be verified, whereas in conference room reviews, opinion takes over from fact, and the people who know the facts are not usually present.

In the time that I worked for Toyota I was very impressed even when high level management visited the plant as all reviews took place on the shop floor and the conditions discussed could be seen and commented on first hand.

In this way not only could a true picture be seen, but practical advice and valuable input could come from the visiting manager, sharing his and other plants experience of similar situations.

Only the final wrap up meeting would take place in a conference room where the visitor would sum up all he had seen and give his more general advice on the plant situation.

With this focus and support, shop floor members feel much more positive about managing problems in the work place and are less likely to allow the problem to deteriorate performance.

They take extraordinary steps to ensure production is maintained, while maintenance and engineering resolve technical problems, something that does not happen in a company that has little shop floor focus.

In these companies the shop floor team will normally stand back until maintenance fixes the problem therefore losing production and inevitably revenue.

One very important feature of an organisation that has Shop Floor Focus is that management rotate through the shop floor teams regularly, carrying out activity reviews using the PDCA format. They do not only turn up when a problem is experienced, but have predetermined reviews even when things are going well. In these circumstances they offer praise and recognition as well as support.

Opposite is an example of shop and group performance visual management boards, they display performance information on the 5 aspects of manufacturing. The information is gathered and displayed on the board by members of the production team. This type of board can be used to display information on any activity. Using this board the supervisor or manager can follow any issues.

The shop board displays the performance of the workshop overall and the results broken down by each group leader "group" in the shop. Trends, as well as performance against targets can be seen for each group. This allows everybody to see which groups are experiencing difficulties, allowing the shop management to provide additional support to those groups.

formance, these items are provided by the teams.

From this board it is easy to see which teams are having the greatest difficulties with their performance. Therefore a visit to the team to review its team board takes you directly to the source of the problem and not one piece of paper has been passed on!

Fig. 10

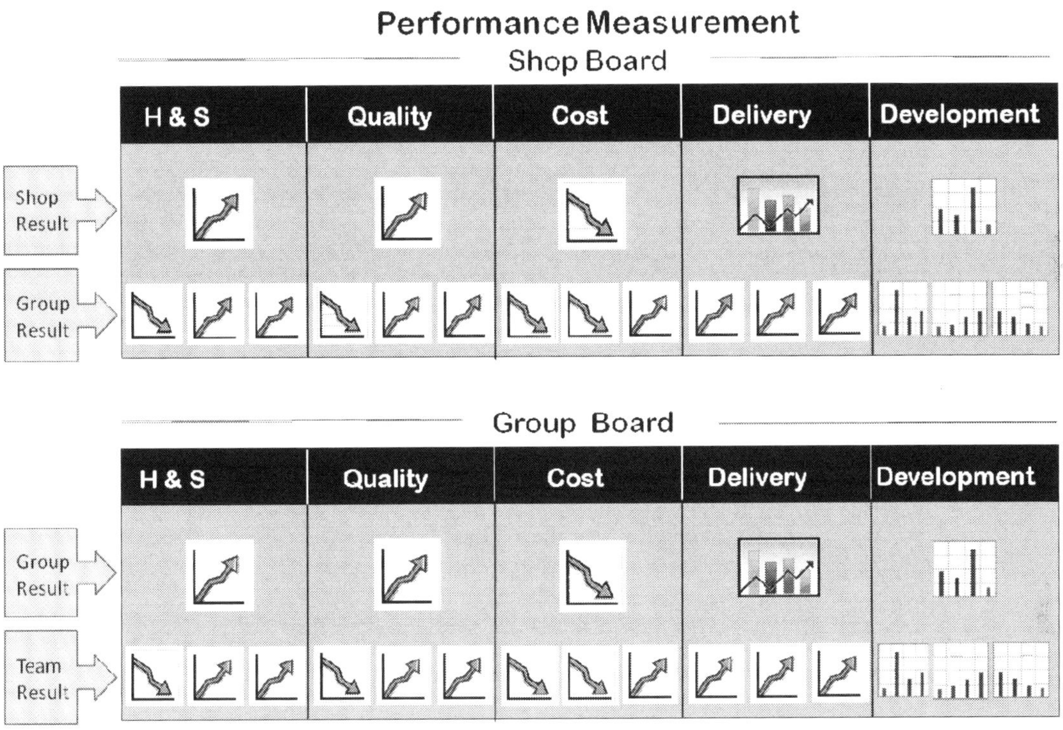

Performance Measurement
Shop Board
Group Board

From the shop board the unit manager can readily see which groups require assistance, this will lead him to the appropriate group board.

The information on these boards is further broken down by each working team. A working team normally consists of 5 members plus a team leader.

Displayed also is a list of the action plans that the group is working on to improve per-

On the team board is displayed all relevant information on the performance difficulties and the investigations in progress. They record concerns by process number, by member and by type of process.

For the concerns tracking system, it is after this step that the escalation process takes over, after the initial investigation by the team indicates they need support. The team then post the concern on the group board to start the support process.

Below is an example of a corresponding team board used to resolve performance issues, the information for this board comes from the group board and the teams investigations. It shows what actions are taking place, any concerns affecting the team and tracks the effectiveness of the activities.

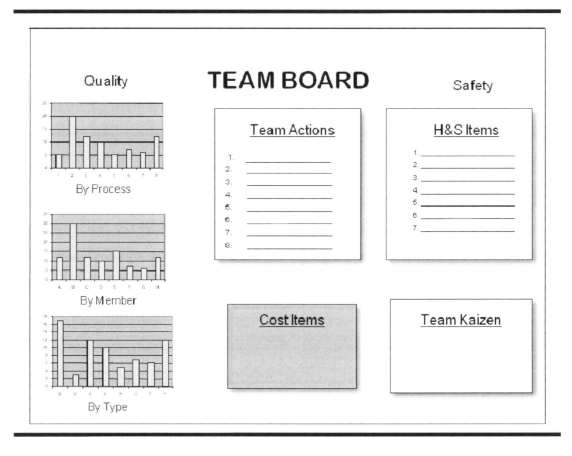

Fig.11

Finally in an organisation that has shop floor focus, there are plans for back up if a piece of equipment fails, the back up ensures production continues and everybody pitches in to assist. Again the focus is providing pre-planned support to the production department to ensure continued revenue stream. There will be more detail provided on this subject later in the book.

Actions

- Make sure everyone in your organisation understands where the revenue is directly generated, how it is generated (what activities) and who is most directly associated with it.

- Ensure that support of this daily revenue generation and its improvement is placed as number one priority throughout the entire organisation.

- Make all aspects of performance and improvement transparent including all activities and concerns by using visual management tools.

- Introduce a management PDCA cycle for following all concerns to ensure timely support is given and nothing stands in the way of improving the business.

- Give autonomy to the shop floor teams to tackle the issues but be ready to provide support, advice and practical solutions when they are stuck.

- Be visible on the shop floor to recognise the effort, provide resources where necessary and listen to the experiences of your people so you can learn how to support more effectively.

5. The Concept Of Challenge

It is very important for a business to be looking ahead while it is carrying out today's production plan and in doing so one must think in terms of how to positively challenge the entire organisation to keep improving.

Value added Vs Non value added work

The figure shown below demonstrates the traditional concept of value added versus non value added work, showing that work consists of value added work, work without value added, and waste.

It is commonly understood that there are 7 types of waste that exist in all activities and these should be the focus of all cost reduction efforts. By listing the actions that take place in a process it is easily seen which of them add value and which contain waste.

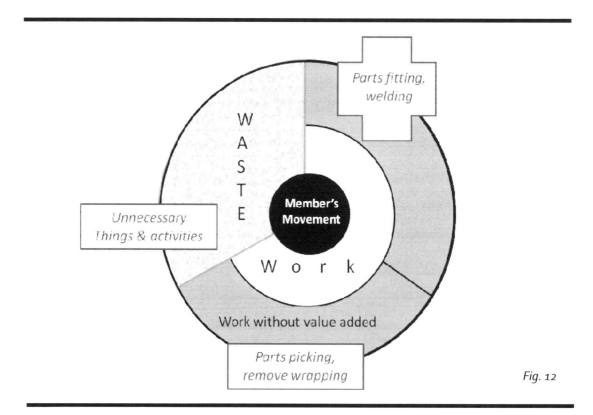

Fig. 12

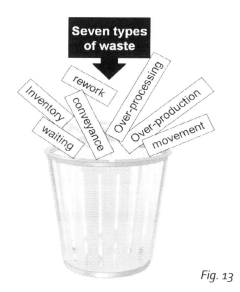

Fig. 13

This however sets the expectation that certain types of non value added are "necessary evils" and are therefore tolerated and even used as excuses not to improve.

To introduce the concept of challenge you need to make a step change in how the workforce thinks of non value added work. They must consider the concept of value added work from the viewpoint of the customer, that is to say "what the customer would expect to pay for".

Consider the following example of non value added and value added work in fitting a screw:

Select the screw – NVA

Pick up screw driver – NVA

Line the screw up to mating part – NVA

Insert screw driver in head of screw – NVA

Tighten screw 16 turns until up to torque – NVA 98% + 2% VA

Return screw driver to holder –NVA

The traditional concept of value added vs non value added would lead us to believe that most of this work, although NVA is necessary.

However from the point of view of the customer he or she should only expect to pay for the screw and the parts it is connecting plus the last 2% of tightening the screw which will prevent any rattle or the screw coming out under use.

Immediately it is obvious that you need to pick the parts up and line everything up, but when you think of it in terms of customer oriented non value added work, the challenge is to reduce its effect by eliminating as much of this activity as possible, instead of just accepting it and passing the cost to the customer.

Can the parts be lined up automatically i.e. designed in such a way that they mate together so the fastener can be introduced without looking?

How far away are the parts stored from the point of fit?

How are they transported to the point of fit?

Already you can see there is a lot of scope for challenging the organisation but lets take the concept of challenge a step further:

So if 15.75 turns of the screw are non value added, can we look for a fastener that gives the same torque results, but can be pushed in or only turned half a revolution?

When you start to think of customer oriented NVA work being waste, you start to realise that the ratio of value added work to non value added activity is in the ratio of 1(va):10,000(nva) a huge opportunity for any organisation. Sadly many organisations do not view added value from the point of the customer and miss the "concept of challenge" thinking that most of the non value added is a necessary evil.

With the correct understanding it is amazing how many cost saving ideas can be generated by an experienced workforce.

A company that satisfies itself with the "status quo" will soon be overtaken and find itself in a fight for survival.

Therefore it is very important that "Kaizen" thinking and the willingness to strive to eliminate ALL waste is necessary for the success of the business (and therefore its people).

This thinking then needs to be integrated with the vision mentioned earlier of where the company is heading so that the workforce understands why it is necessary to be challenged. This is "The Concept of Challenge".

Challenge through Business Plan Deployment

Challenge targets must be built into the annual business plan preferably using Business Plan Deployment techniques, so that every one has had input and that real actions are identified to try to achieve the targets.

To visualise the plan and integrate it into an easily understood tracking system it is advisable to use the **P**lan – **D**o – **C**heck - **A**ction format that identifies where the plan is not working and calls for a countermeasure action plan to get back on target (see page 28).

A regular PDCA review must take place to follow progress of these activities, recognition during these reviews must be given for good progress and support must be given immediately for the items the team is struggling with, absolutely no blame should be attached if a team is struggling to reach one of its challenge targets.

Progress towards the challenge targets must be very visible to all members of the organisation, as information but also as recognition where progress is good and where more organisational support is required.

It is important that management recognise that their job is to provide the resources; time, materials, budget and labour on a timely basis as required.

Example:
A well known vehicle manufacturer wanted to introduce a new model range to be manufactured somewhere in Europe, but within an existing plant as they did not wish to add the overhead of a new plant to their costs.

All of the European Plants were informed of the situation and they were advised of the performance criteria they had to achieve by the decision date in 3 years time to be considered for the product line.

Each of the Plants provided the vision and an outline of what needed to be done to become "The Chosen Plant".

Adding an extra product line would secure the future of the Plant and greatly enhance the ability to keep up performance even when some models were coming to the end of their life.

The vision and outline plans were shared with the workforce and the first years "Challenge" was set, using BPD to establish the viability of the targets and identify the activities that would take place to achieve them.

Members on the shop floor were consulted for their ideas to achieve the targets and all ideas were considered with the practical plans being submitted. This activity generated many ideas for improvement and in the first year the opportunity to soundly beat the challenge targets.

The theme continued during the annual planning for the 3 years and with progress updates everyone understood why the targets were set as they were. There were no surprises with sudden out of the blue targets no one understood. Consistency was maintained as the plans unfolded and, as everyone saw the results they knew what had to be done.

The plans were not the same in every plant as some plants had to overcome disadvantages others did not have, and vice versa. However a clear leader emerged and the European organisation determined how to convey the results without de-motivating the other plants.

Considerable effort went into the communication with recognition given to what they had achieved and a very clear explanation of why the successful plant was chosen. This is not to say that there was no disappointment, but the enthusiasm of the workforce was maintained through the fact that they at least shared benefits generated by their improvements even if they didn't win the ultimate prize.

They also benefited from working for a truthful and thoughtful organisation which could communicate in an empathetic manner.

The following year when the theme "strengthening the organisation" was used for the challenge, people enthusiastically participated. I believe the main factor for this was the fact that people did not feel that the challenge was dumped on them, but that everyone worked together to achieve the goals.

The challenge, if not quite fun to do, develops new skills, stimulates interesting activities and ensures that the total organisation supports the improvement efforts.

In chapter 11, I will explain how to engage shop floor members in driving Business Plan Deployment activities as part of their development.

Actions

- Make sure you have a very clear vision of your business for the next 3-5 years and the year by year challenges to get there.

- Ensure everyone in the organisation understands where the company is going and what it is going to take to get there as well as the benefits for the work force.

- Determine how you will share the benefits; what can the company afford to pay its people for the improvement results? (Annual bonus?)

- Educate your organisation on the concept of challenge (new VA—NVA thinking) and stretch targets and their link to an annual success bonus.

- Implement a BPD activity to involve everyone in the effort.

- Implement a PDCA management cycle activity to follow progress and ensure that support is available when teams start to miss the stretch targets.

- Ensure the PDCA reviews recognise the successful activities.

6. Roles and Responsibilities

Balancing the roles of the organisation

In Part I, we have identified the requirements for setting the right environment by having a vision, establishing production principles, setting a strategy to involve and empower the workforce to achieve the vision through Business Plan Deployment.

We have also discussed the importance of having a set of beliefs and Values to drive the behaviours of everyone in the organisation.

But like all good teams we don't want everyone trying to do everything, like a group of schoolboys chasing the football all over the pitch in a football match.

A professional football team consists of different types of players with different skills; the goalkeeper who needs to be quick and agile, full backs who need to be strong and a good tackler, midfield players who need to be able to tackle, dribble the ball and accurately pass to a forward and of course the forwards who must be quick and agile with the ball and hopefully have a powerful kick for shooting at goal.

This is the most obvious team in a professional football club but there is a support team that works behind the scenes to ensure the footballers only have to worry about their performance on the football pitch.

The members of the support team; Chairman (owner), Team manager, coaching team, club doctor / physiotherapist and scouts, each have their own particular role to play.

So you can see the team is more than the players. Teamwork has to go from top to bottom of the organisation with each level having its particular contribution to make. In the best football clubs these boundaries are very well understood and the chairman resists the urge to select the team for the manager!

This is the same with a business; it is important to ensure that the various activities are carried out at the right level of the organisation.

Typically in large organisations managers are carrying out much of the work that their direct reports should be taking responsibility for.

In many cases the managers do not understand the various levels of responsibility and who should be doing what. These organisations usually have quite involved Roles and Responsibility documentation , which invariably has most people overlapping their responsibilities, so if one doesn't do something hopefully someone else will pick it up.

The figure opposite is a handy tool for checking whether your organisation has the right balance within its activities. It shows basically where the responsibility lays with the various aspects of running the business and each level becomes the focal point for ensuring these activities are understood and carried out.

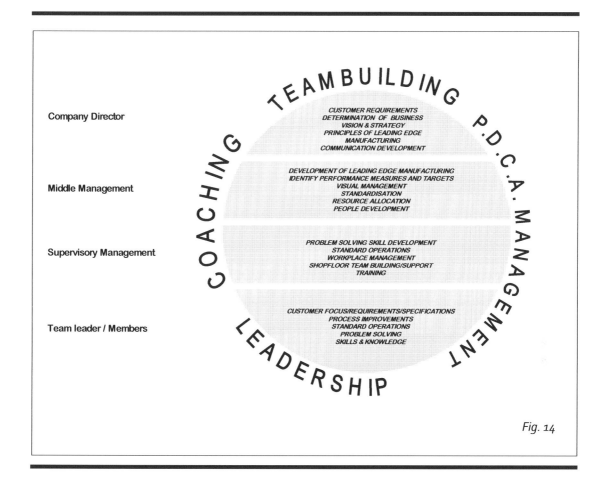

Fig. 14

Role of Company Director

The Company Director takes on the responsibility for understanding his customers requirements, which he must convert to an appropriate vision and strategy that will achieve them.

He must lead benchmarking externally, to identify appropriate principles of leading edge manufacturing systems, that would enable the company to obtain an operating advantage over its competitors.

This must be communicated as an absolute requirement of the forward vision, and the complete management team must be educated in these concepts so that they can train the people who report to them. This will en-

sure that the workforce gets the message loud and clear of the future direction of the company.

Too often C.E.O.'s of companies hear of an operating concept and thinking it a good idea, request that supervisors are trained to roll out the new concept.

They then expect the middle and upper management to intuitively support the implementation of concepts they are not familiar with, and which often conflicts with traditional wisdom ingrained over many years into the upper management team.

With the model above the total management team will be engaged in the roll out of new concepts avoiding this clash.

Basically company directors create the requirement of new concepts, middle management learn about them and develop an implementation strategy, first line supervisors learn about the new concepts and organise and carry out knowledge and skills training to support the implementation strategy.

It is the responsibility of the company director to develop a communication strategy so that the complete organisation can understand the vision and strategy of the company and why it is important.

He must ensure that benefits are clearly identified and the communication process must be two ways such that open honest communication takes place about the areas of difficulty.

This should not be a one off communication but should be the beginning of an ongoing process which takes the pulse of the organisation and therefore avoids conflicts building up.

This strategy should also recognise that the vision will need to change over time and that keeping everybody in the information circle will guide the business to success.

Role of Middle Management

It is middle management's role, supported by specialists, to develop the leading edge technology and production system principles for integration into the companies system of production.

They must develop the appropriate Key Performance Indicators that will quickly identify progress of the activities towards the vision as well as the impact on daily operating performance.

It can be expected that changes might bring a temporary slip in current performance due to

mastering new concepts, so visual management must be used to track and ensure performance quickly comes back under control.

They must also take responsibility for making these Key Performance Indicators highly visible in the workplace so everyone can see how well they are progressing. They must drive the process for identifying support needs and activities when adverse results are experienced.

For ensuring consistent decisions and actions middle management must also develop the concept of standardisation within the company, that is to say: how to standardise performance measurement, performance reviews, and the company problem solving process as well as standardised operations. They will also have to standardise the methods of communications to support the managing director's communication strategy.

By having one method to identify problems and resolve them the workforce will quickly develop understanding and speedy reactions to all adverse situations. This will over time facilitate better communication and increase the understanding of the workforce.

One world class company uses an A3 sheet developed into a problem solving format, such that from the problem statement through to the countermeasure is contained on one structured sheet. This facilitates the understanding of the problem and assists the storage of the information for future use should the problem re-occurr. Also problems or challenges are all structured in the same way for easy understanding by the complete organisation.

Middle management must ensure that resources are available as they are required, in particular they may need to share labour across the company to support the various stages of implementation.

This must be done selflessly developing a

sense of the whole organisation being one big team and avoiding employing short term people that are not really required.

Coupled with this idea of resource sharing should be making opportunities for people development. The middle managers should be positively engaged in ensuring development opportunities are identified for all levels of the organisation.

Preparing the next levels of management is important but they should not forget the development laterally of people who may not be capable of becoming managers. These people should also have personal development opportunities up to their level of capability. On many occasions these are missed by traditional thinking companies; we will develop this theme later in the book.

Role of Supervisory Management

Supervisory Management have the responsibility for ensuring that workforce knowledge and skills are suitably updated, to support the implementation of leading edge production principles developed by middle management such as: Just in Time, standardised operations, total Productive Maintenance, problem solving etc.

They must ensure that appropriate training is properly carried out to enable the workforce to move from awareness through understanding into capability to perform. Many such concepts die early in their lives because the workforce never moves beyond awareness and therefore never develops the skills to sustain the activity.

It is supervisory management's responsibility to ensure the workforce understands the production output required, the customer's requirements and the assembly/quality speci-

fications of the product. He is responsible for the output of his group and also for enhancing performance through process improvement, standardised operations application, good problem solving and enhanced knowledge & skills.

Although these roles clearly show the different responsibilities of each level, strategically the supervisor's role is central to achieving member involvement and sustainability, which is what this book is all about! This level of management can either reinforce the vision developed by higher management or can conversely destroy all faith in it.

So it is obligatory that we stop for a moment and dive deeper into the elements of the supervisor's activities, in order to understand what is needed from our supervisors to create a successful and sustainable improvement environment.

As the main point of contact between the management team and the workforce is affected through the role of the supervisor, how the supervisor behaves and talks will inevitably affect the way that the company management team is perceived.

Therefore it is crucial that this role is understood not only in terms of Roles and Responsibilities but also practices, behaviours and relationships within the organisation. The front line supervisor will play a key role, in whether the workforce applies the production system principles and whether they will have faith in the visual management support systems available.

He has to be confident in the way that he demonstrates good management practices and applies company rules and agreements, but at the same time has to understand the dynamics of the workplace.

It is important that as well as being seen as a person of experience and authority he is also seen as a father figure.

He needs to demonstrate care and consideration for those who work for him, providing appropriate support, sometimes even for non work issues an individual might be experiencing in his personal life.

The supervisor also needs to be passionate in leading his group to carry out continuous daily improvement, to meet the targets set to achieve customer satisfaction and business growth.

All of this sounds great but how does it translate into concrete actions that you and your supervisor can develop and improve upon?

First your selection of supervisor must consider very carefully his ability to reason with people and his capacity to explain concepts and fundamentals in an easily understood manner.

He needs a firm grasp of the Business Fundamentals and Production System principles such that he can demonstrate their importance and benefits.

He should have a track record of working with the workforce during which he will have been able to demonstrate his knowledge, experience and trustworthiness. This will develop a natural respect for him built on his abilities and integrity, not on his status.

This does not happen by chance so middle management must have a development plan that identifies likely candidates early in their careers so that they can have assignments that teaches them all of the skill sets mentioned above.

Remember supervisors are the key to how much improvement you will make in your business, through their ability to engage the workforce in positive activities to make op-

erational improvements and therefore much needed cost savings.

Typically in Lean manufacturing companies the supervisor will have at least 10 years service before he becomes a supervisor, with several years as a team leader. The benefits are enormous when a supervisor is respected and trusted by his group because of his experience and knowledge. His interventions are accepted without question and his guidance is welcomed by the group. He is considered to be a wise leader and father figure.

Normally a supervisor would not be hired from outside of the company.

Five key elements of front line supervisor 's role

There are 5 elements of the supervisor's role which if carried out properly will result in having a workforce that understands its role, can skilfully carry it out, and feels appreciated for the effort it is making.

The objectives of the front line supervisor fall broadly into two categories :

. *"achieving production targets"* and
. *"educating and developing their staff"*
   (team leaders and members)

Achieving production targets can only be achieved consistently with a well informed, skill-full workforce, who through the leadership skills of the frontline supervisor will be motivated to engage in daily activities to improve company performance.

5 KEY ELEMENTS OF THE FRONT LINE SUPERVISOR

Fig. 15

As we look inside the objectives circle we see that there are five elements of the front-line supervisor's work that must be developed to achieve these two objectives.

Standard Operations

Standard operations are the bedrock of an efficient production system that produces high quality products. Without them your processes are built on shifting sand. They provide the ability to smoothly perform an operation within a consistent cycle time and with a method that has been proven to assure the health and safety of those performing them as well as the integrity of the product.

Therefore the first key element of the front-line supervisor's job is to establish, manage and improve regularly "Standard Operations".

When goods are produced without the use of

properly documented standard operations it is impossible to manage quality, carry out improvements, or solve problems.

Without them, people can not be properly trained in a consistent method, therefore the method will change every time it is performed.

No one will know how the operation was performed in the event of a quality defect, therefore problem solving will not be possible. Needless to say with an operation with no defined method, improvement will be impossible to establish or sustain.

Therefore the role of the frontline supervisor must be to work with his teams to establish proper standardised methods for each operation such that quality can be assured every time the operation is carried out. Only the teams with their team leader can establish the standard operations including the "knacks" to be applied to ensure correct results.

The supervisor must coach the teams in documenting the standards and how to train properly from standard operation sheets. He signs off every standard operation in his group.

He then needs to set up a daily review by the team leader to ensure the standard operation is being applied. He must follow up each time the standard is not applied to understand why and what needs to be done to ensure compliance.

Based on standards for process design, the supervisor should coach and encourage the team leader with his team to look for improvement opportunities in the standard operation. He should ensure that they document changes properly and re-train all individuals in the new standard operation.

Changes should be based on eliminating waste and removing difficulties to make the standard operation easier to apply.

For all quality defects, the start point for problem solving must always be the standard operation confirmation. In many cases the defect will be as a result of the standard operation not being applied.

Of course abnormalities do occasionally occurr that cause the member to break the standard operation; this can be identified by the member that was carrying out the operation at the time of the defect. The abnormality must be counter-measured immediately to prevent re-occurrence.

PDCA management practices

The second element is to develop PDCA practices within his group so that all members of the workforce get into the habit of **(P)** planning their actions, **(D)** carrying them out as planned, **(C)** reviewing them regularly during the activity to ensure that not only is the action taking place as planned, but that the results progress is in line with expectations, **(A)** if they are not as expected further actions must be immediately identified to improve the situation.

Quite often teams have good intentions but can not seem to get round to carrying out the actions that are needed, or fail to realise that the results are falling below those needed for success, which is why the PDCA cycle used as a daily follow activity is so important.

When the group manages their activities in this way they do not need a manager to come and tell them that the results are not effective. Instead the manager's role becomes one of reviewing how he can help the group catch back.

This moves the management team away from being critics to being a positive support team and also allows them to give recognition when the plan is working.

It also demonstrates trust in the workforce based on a practical action model.

The use of group/team boards coupled to PDCA visual management process will get the workforce into the habit of reviewing their activities and taking corrective action where necessary without waiting to be told to do so.

It is important that the supervisor reviews his group's performance problems regularly using the PDCA format and uses the concerns tracking system to provide external support quickly when ever it is needed.

Skill development and flexibility

The third element is to ensure that all members of the group are developing their operational skills, and that there is sufficient flexibility in the group to manage their processes even when suffering from member absence.

It can be demoralising if the same one or two persons have to take on the most difficult operations when absence occurs, so the spreading of operational skills is of primary importance to the front line supervisor.

In moving line and cell assembly processes, the cycle time of the process is governed by the demand of the product and the operations although repetitive, require the application of certain basic skills.

For example installing screws at varying angles of inclination rapidly, or installing weather strips/hot melt wax requiring considerable dexterity of wrist and finger movement.

Poor mastery of basic skills will result in the member cutting corners on other aspects of the operation to keep up with production, resulting in poor quality and increased costs of repair. In some cases it can also cause repetitive strain injury which could have a lifetime effect on the member.

Therefore the front line supervisor must ensure that the workforce is trained thoroughly in these basic skills off line before they are faced with a stressful situation trying to keep up with the speed of the line. The training must be "one on one" with the team leader who should demonstrate how to do complete with all knacks to ease the process and the member should be given the opportunity to practice and then demonstrate his ability.

This should be checked not only by the team leader but also by the supervisor against a standard, prior to the member going on line to work.

It is critical that the front line supervisor reviews constantly not only additional operations for members but also if the basic skills continue to be applied smoothly and easily. Quite often this can be an early sign of a developing member problem such as poor posture or incorrect use of tooling causing fatigue or strains.

The operation training programme is a key element for managing safety, quality, output and cost and as such should be structured to teach the operation and skills in a highly structured format. It is very important that the front line supervisor ensures that his team leaders understand and follow the structured format.

The components to be assembled should be introduced to the member with an explanation of the function of the parts and the critical items to look for when assembling.

This should be broken down by explaining each *major step* of the operation, its appropriate *key point* to look for during the step and the *key point reason* (why it is an important point- what the effect of not applying the key point will be). When people understand why the key point is important they normally take greater care.

Each major step should be demonstrated by the team leader and then tried by the member who should recite the major step, key point and key point reason as he does the operation. Any mistakes should be corrected immediately.

When the trainee has demonstrated his understanding of the operation he should be allowed to practice on his own for a period, after which the team leader should return and review his progress. When the team leader is satisfied with the demonstration (including reciting major step, key point, key point reason) he will call the supervisor to review progress and for the decision to move the trainee to the assembly line for on line coaching.

67

During times of product changes when the training effort will be high, the front line supervisor will identify a training team from within the team leader organisation. This team becomes known as "master trainers" who take on the responsibility of training the workforce in the new operations. This not only structures the training but also gives an opportunity to recognise the more skillful team leaders.

A skills matrix should be displayed on the group board to demonstrate the flexibility of the group; also to indicate who should receive training next, to spread the skills evenly in the group.

The skills matrix for each team can be expanded to strategise how to share members between teams to create the greatest flexibility and member interest.

The front line supervisor must also develop his group in non functional skills which will help them in managing their own performance; these types of skills will be explained in part III of this book.

Abnormality Management

The fourth element is to develop the groups understanding of abnormality management and how to solve these problems. Abnormality management means to manage situations that could result in a failure sooner than waiting for the failure to occur and then taking action.

An example of this could be, when a member has a re-occurring problem on the line and keeps encroaching on the work place of another member, increasing the potential that the other member will make a mistake. So before a mistake happens the group will solve the member's problem and avoid the encroachment and the potential of two costly errors.

The start point for abnormality management must be with improving the workplace organisation through good 5S practice. The frontline supervisor must take the lead role working with his group to have a clean, tidy and safe workplace.

In conjunction with this the front line supervisor must introduce the concept of visual management to enable the team to see abnormal conditions.

Marking out the workplace showing the planned location of workstations, materials and tooling is one example of visual management. In this way the group can easily and quickly recognise when items are out of place, or a process is out of station.

In coupling standardisation and visual management, out of standard conditions (abnormalities) can instantly be corrected before accidents or quality issues occur.

The various standards for the group must therefore be made visual and a process of checking against them established by the group, these standards should include; health & safety, quality, delivery, cost, fixture & equipment maintenance, 5S etc.

An additional benefit from this is that the group will, over time, become much more pro-active in its thinking and approach to its various activities.

Finally to be able to react to the visual management, the frontline supervisor must develop the problem solving skills of his work group to enable them to discover the root cause and introduce an effective countermeasure that will last.

Cultivating a good production environment

The fifth element is the element that enables the other four to achieve a level of sustainable success; this level will depend entirely on how positive the production environment is perceived by the workforce.

Please remember the old adage which states that: *"Perception is reality"!*

It's not management's perception that counts. This is the element which most "technocratic" type management teams miss out, then wonder why the performance improvements (cost savings) are so small and take so much effort!

The frontline supervisor plays a key role in establishing an environment where team working flourishes, where inter-level and inter-departmental relationships are positive, and where the true measure is what's best for the company and its employees.

He must effectively manage the welfare of his group, personally taking an interest in their wellbeing, and must manage them in a firm but fair manner in matters relating to company rules or agreements.

Every day he should greet each member of his workgroup individually and check whether they have any concerns needing his assistance. Should a member have a concern the frontline manager after greeting everyone, and setting the work for the day, should return to the individual to understand what the problem is and what he can do to help.

For example if the individual is suffering from a strain or other type of injury sustained at home the evening before, the supervisor should make immediate arrangements for him/her to visit the company medical department for investigation. In this way the supervisor displays concern for his group members and acts very much as a parent or a good friend would.

In industry there are many opportunities to suffer strains either from poor ergonomically designed processes or poor operator posture.

The supervisor must ensure proper consideration is given during product and process design to good ergonomics.

He should then subsequently ensure that good posture is included in all training activities.

Team leaders should check their processes every day, to look for cases of poor operator posture, caused by poor concentration or abnormalities causing the member to rush.

In cases of poor posture the member should be retrained in the correct posture for the process.

When a member complains of suffering a strain from a process, the member should immediately be taken off of that process and given a process with different posture to rest the strain. The team should then investigate with the injured member a proper posture for the process and they should be re-trained. The member should go back on the process when the strain has improved and should be monitored closely by the group leader for any re-occurrence.

In this way the supervisor demonstrates his commitment to the welfare of the members of his group.

He must develop the team working in his group by coaching and encouraging them to come up with their own solutions to issues where ever possible. He must however ensure that support is given whenever the group can not resolve an issue.

Many complaints are made by shop floor people because the supervisor is too busy to help with a problem in a timely manner, therefore the use of a visual concerns tracking process with automatic escalation is vital. This will ensure the management team becomes quickly involved in supporting the supervisor when he is overwhelmed, thus avoiding the workforce feeling neglected.

The supervisor needs to have a communication system supported by the entire management team that provides him with the time and opportunity to listen to his workgroup and be able to respond to them openly and honestly.

World class companies identify times in the working day when the supervisor can carry out specific communications with his group, typically these are:

5 minutes prior to the start of production shift.

5 minutes at the end of the morning tea/ coffee break.

Lunch break meetings.

15-30 minutes after the finish of the shift.

The group leader must be able to call on higher levels of management, to attend communication sessions with members of the workforce so that they can understand any concerns and to ensure that all parties are fully informed on any issues that are outstanding.

When there is doubt about a situation the supervisor should always refer the item to the manager of the area, he should seek an accurate answer and be prepared to share it honestly even if it will not be popular.

Of course sensitive competitive information must be managed carefully. This should be explained to the workforce if it prevents full disclosure. They will normally understand if management's integrity is intact.

The frontline supervisor must work with his group to ensure a safe and healthy work environment is maintained, developing it as a joint responsibility by encouraging teams to carry out their own audits and coming up with solutions.

He should also encourage them to play an active role whenever one of the members has an accident or a near miss. He should empower the team member who had the accident to lead the problem solving activity with the group so that the member can confirm the solution as good.

The frontline supervisor must be the leader of shop floor consensus decision making, he should explain the key criteria used for making decisions and should encourage the group to come to a decision on operating issues using this criteria.

At the same time he must ensure that every voice is heard if people have opposing opinions on a subject.

On the majority of occasions a solution will grow out of the consensus decision making process but sometimes there will be more than one possible solution.

Because of this the supervisor should take the time to evaluate properly all suggested solutions, measuring them against the criteria so that all participants can see why one solution is preferable to another.

The people whose ideas are not being implemented must be able to understand why and buy into the chosen solution; there can not be a vote!

The thing to bear in mind here is that the more decisions made by the workforce the more support they will give to ensuring any planned actions are successful.

You can considerably reduce the risk of bad decisions by ensuring your frontline supervisor coaches the application of the criteria and does not allow "not invented here" or other equally negative thinking to influence the group decision.

The final part of a good production environment is ensuring that there is recognition for people who achieve good results as well as recognising actions taken by individuals that demonstrate good citizenship.

Good citizenship is when people recognise abnormal situations and take action to ensure that others are not put at risk because of a safety issue, or that quality is not compromised by substandard workmanship.

When people receive recognition they feel positive about themselves, what they are doing and about every one around them.

This inspires good team working and an open honest environment.

In chapter 8 of this book we will review some of the ways that recognition can be given.

Training the Supervisor in his role

I hope by now you see how key the supervisor's role is in guiding his group and encouraging them positively to become involved in various aspects of the business, while at the same time fostering a caring environment that demonstrates that each member is an integral part of the company team.

When considering how to train the supervisor in carrying out his tasks it is a good idea to break the tasks up into pre-shift preparation, start up tasks, on going daily tasks and end of shift tasks.

In doing this you should create a timing chart that can be easily ticked daily by the supervisor to show what he managed to get done and what did not get done. This will enable you to review with him the road-blocks that prevent him working with his people as he should.

From this you can agree actions to help him free himself up to get these tasks done, because frankly they are the most important tasks in the management organisation.

On occasions it may be necessary to retrain group leaders. Often called "Back to Basics" this can be for many reasons but is even necessary when a group leader moves from one department to another.

In this case the training should be done in a block period while others manage the daily activity of running his group.

If there is more than one shift operating it is also beneficial to bring the opposite shift supervisor into the training. In this way they learn together and benefit from synergy between the shifts when they return to the group.

The training activity should allow the supervisor to try out the activities trained and he should gradually take over the tasks as the training progresses.

In carrying out the training in this manner it gives the supervisor time to work on the skills with the trainer, practice them and obtain feedback from the trainer on real life actions not class room theory.

Actions

- Review the objectives and role of your frontline supervisors to determine whether the 5 elements are clearly stated in the description.

- Establish the basis for developing the 5 elements ensuring that you have previously set your vision and Beliefs and Values.

- Set up training programmes for your supervisors on any of the 5 elements they are not fully familiar with.

- Introduce the 5 elements with additional required training but ensure the supervisor is most knowledgeable about these items to ensure his position is respected.

- Ensure the complete management team fully supports the supervisor group in all of these activities particularly with consensus decision making and communication.

Role of Team Leader / Member

The role of the team leaders and members must also be clearly defined and understood.

First the team members must understand customer requirements in terms of Quality, Cost and Delivery and they must be focussed on surpassing these requirements in their daily work activity.

They must be encouraged to look out for sub-standard parts or work not only from their team but from earlier processes and to report these immediately to their team leader or supervisor (ways to encourage will be discussed later).

They must be trained to understand the quality standards and the effect on the customer of failure to reach that standard; they must apply the concept of challenge to ensure customer satisfaction.

As "Standardised Operations" are the best way to ensure quality, the team members must focus on carrying them out properly and where ever possible look for ways to improve them (eliminating waste).

Daily improvement of processes and operations must be an important part of the job of the team member and support must be given by the team leader and supervisor to help the member make improvements.

There is no one else in the organisation with the same in depth knowledge of the operations; consequently the member must become a key problem solver.

The team member must therefore learn how to carry out a standardised problem solving process to find the root cause for operational problems.

The most important assets of the organisation are the skills and knowledge of the workforce and ways must be found to harness them for the daily improvement of the processes and product.

This is why the management team must always be on the look out for developing more skills in the team members and involving them in activities that allow them to use their knowledge.

Because of this knowledge team members should participate in activities not focussed on their assembly operations but on broader aspects of their working environment. These activities are introduced in chapters 11 & 12.

Team leaders must ensure that all of their team members understand their particular roles within the team, especially which operations they will be trained in to create the greatest flexibility possible for the team and the group.

The team leader must carry out the specific training required for the members to master all the operations indentified.

He must be skilled in identifying where members are not carrying out the operations as trained, to ensure additional training is given before a member suffers a strain injury or creates poor quality product.

He must also create a team atmosphere within the members by ensuring they are kept informed of issues and their opinion is sought before actions are determined.

The team leader should always be on the look out for any potential problems the members might experience, he should always be on hand to support and resolve the problems.

It is important that the team leader leads by example, therefore he must be fully conversant with all operations in the team and must be prepared to help members if a situation causes them to struggle. He should always react to difficulties in a very positive manner, being first to offer help, and to act as a catalyst for identifying countermeasures.

Once the appropriate Roles and Responsibilities are defined for each level of the organisation they must be aligned with the terms and conditions of employment. When a person signs a contract with the company he must fully understand what is required of him.

When the company expectations are included in the terms and conditions of employment and clearly explained during the recruitment process, it enables the company and the Trade Union to jointly explain the thinking and "company culture" utilised to create a successful company which is able to support its workforce in all aspects of the relationship.

Actions

- Review how clear the Roles and Responsibilities are for your organisation. Are they too complicated and do they overlap?

- Review whether they make it clear what each level of the organisation should be providing for the other levels.

- Re-write your company roles and responsibilities making it clear where the responsibility really lies for each major activity; do not share responsibility across levels.

- Make sure that opportunities are identified to engage team members in wider aspects of the business through such activities as quality circles or business plan deployment. (Different ideas are introduced in Part III, chapter 11)

- Ensure that your terms and conditions of employment support the actions required by the Roles and Responsibilities definitions.

Roles & Responsibilities

7. Open Communication

The annual report drove everybody crazy!

Good communication is so important.

Communication is often a much ignored management practice, that is handled so badly, it undoes all of the good intentions of the management team.

It is a subject as important as having a well defined Production System to operate with.

Traditional communication training focuses on listening, talking, observation, handling negative re-actions and persuasion skills which are all very important.

But what is normally missing is the strategy of why we want to communicate. What is the reason for acquiring all of these skills?

Each communication event is treated like a one off communication activity instead of part of an overall strategy.

Surely the objective is to make good communication a daily activity for everyone in the organisation, developing an openness that fosters healthy respect and friendship.

When we communicate we should be trying to develop a relationship between the workforce and management, as opposed to just keeping people informed about what we are doing and listening for any signs of resistance we must overcome.

If everyone including management makes their decisions based on agreed "business needs criteria", it will be clear for all to see that decisions are taken for the good of all.

If this is the case, then a communication strategy can be developed to improve openness and trust between the workforce and the management team, as well as keeping everyone informed.

Communication Strategy

It is absolutely vital that you keep your people fully informed about the performance of the company and its competitors, about any investments in progress and information on any particularly difficult problems the company is facing.

The more informed the workforce is the better they will understand the actions of the company and therefore be in a position to be involved.

I have experienced several occasions when due to the lack of transparency, members of the workforce have felt helpless over pending decisions that will affect them,. They have just had to wait and see what happens.

May be if there had been more open communication, the workforce could have seen the problem coming and been part of a positive solution.

The communication must be two way on all subjects even when only passing on a high level operational decision.

You should plan to have a quarterly presentation for the complete workforce on the state of the business. As this is one way information sharing, a mass presentation or showing of a video message would be appropriate, as long as it is followed by a short questionnaire to ensure you are informed of any parts of the presentation that were not understood. By doing this it gives you the opportunity to follow up with clarification.

Feedback must be sought on potential problems foreseen by the decision, open discussion must take place about the concern and what can be done to countermeasure the problem.

The workforce must not be ignored if their reaction is not as positive as that expected. Consideration must be given to the fact that they will almost always have a slightly different perspective than management.

In fact that is what makes their input so valuable.

They are at the front line of any production decision and have more experience of reality in production than any one.

Time must be taken to thoroughly explore their reactions to the decision in view of the business needs criteria. If the high level decision is in line with the criteria this must be explained clearly to the workforce.

Discussions must then take place about their objections, to discover what is driving the concern and to see if implementation can be carried out in a manner that builds more workforce confidence in the decision, *e.g.*

regular reviews during implementation.

When objections are about imagined outcomes or impact on the workforce by implementing the decision, action to monitor the impact/success factors should be introduced to support the decision implementation.

This will demonstrate that although you may not agree, at least you are taking their view point seriously. In this way you will start to develop a relationship founded on openness and respect for each others viewpoint.

Over time as the workforce gains more confidence in your decisions, the objections will decline and a more positive feeling will be developed in the workforce.

Your communication strategy should include how your group leaders keep their groups informed on performance progress and any potential hazard situations that might arise.

A good method for this is to have a group meeting adjacent to the group performance board every shift for 5 minutes before the start of shift.

During this time the group leader goes through their last shift performance and identifies what needs to be improved. He also informs them of any carry over points from the opposite shift and of any health and safety points to be aware of. It also allows any member to raise a concern he or she might need assistance on during the shift.

In addition leading lean manufacturers also allow an extra 5 minutes following the morning tea/coffee break for company and local information sessions delivered by the group leader. Each day is assigned a topic typically as follows:

On *Mondays* will be feedback on last weeks local shop performance in H&S, Quality, Delivery, Cost & resource development and giving information on any special activities for this week.This will be put together by the unit manager and delivered by the group leaders.

On *Tuesdays* information is shared from the company on organisation/procedural or system problems or changes planned to take place. This will be put together by HR Planning and delivered by the group leaders.

On *Wednesdays* overall plant performance is explained, any short falls by workshop and information concerning any special actions being undertaken will be shared. This will be put together by production planning and delivered by the group leaders.

On *Thursdays* Health & Safety instruction is given alternated every other week with group audits of their area. The instruction will come from company H&S instruction sheets delivered by the group leaders and the audit will be carried out by all members led by the group leaders.

On *Fridays* there will be a group review of the top concern relating to operating performance and on this day recognition ceremonies will take place instead of the concern review if required. (Recognition ceremonies will be explained later in the book).

By using this process there is a constant stream of information flowing from the organisation to the workforce such that if there are questions they can easily be taken up at the communication sessions mentioned in this chapter

Promoting two way communication

However having a communication strategy is more than determining how you are going to keep your employees informed it should also allow them to keep you informed.

A good communication strategy ensures that there are also many opportunities for your people to inform you of their concerns, thoughts and ideas. These opportunities should range from casual conversation, organised opinion gathering, and having a structured concerns follow process that allows concerns to be escalated through the organisation for resolution.

Let's look more in depth at each of these opportunities:

The not so casual- Casual Conversation

This can happen in a couple of ways, first encourage your people to talk with you when you visit the work area,. For example drop in on a team during tea break, buy them a coffee and ask their opinion about projects that are underway or in the pipeline.

What is it that concerns them about the way the company is operating?

What's going well and not so well? Check their understanding of the business plan. Become a fisherman, trawling for the real hot issues, but do not use this opportunity to defend issues, because you want people to be open and react honestly to your questions.

Defending makes people nervous that maybe they said the wrong thing, instead offer to look into their concerns and promise to get back to them.

Lunch Box Meetings

The second way to do this is to arrange lunch time sessions to meet with groups, provide lunch for them and then listen. Lunch box sessions should be held regularly with all levels of the organisation taking part.

Encourage them to discuss issues that are important to them, be prepared to discuss openly your point of view. In these sessions it is ok to correct misunderstandings and explore why you have a different opinion to the group.

These sessions will provide valuable insight into what your workforce thinks about the important company issues.

Do they see management as self serving or supportive?

They will bring a different perspective on the issues and you may discover that what you thought was the burning issue is not for the workforce.

You will be surprised at how many issues are floating about which in reality are easy to resolve but always seem to escape the attention of management.

In these lunch time sessions it is important to have good open discussion and to take immediate follow up action to ensure these issues are entered into the concerns tracking system.

To get as broad a picture as possible different meetings should be held with teams, random groups of people, team leaders and group leaders. From this you get several different perspectives on the same problem, maybe demonstrating why issues do not always get resolved.

It doesn't matter whether an answer is immediately available for those points raised during the meeting, you can always ask for time to investigate and report back. But an immediate reaction can be a powerful motivator if you empathise with the point and sincerely promise to return with a more considered response after some investigation.

NB. It is however very important that you do return with an answer and not forget!

Concerns resolution process

The concerns resolution process described on page 49 is a very important system for two way communication which has the benefit of making visible all of the issues and concerns in the workplace. It not only communicates the issue but also demonstrates the ability of the organisation to resolve them quickly or not as the case may be, in a way that is easy for everyone to see and understand.

The concerns resolution process is also the nucleus for dealing with concerns raised at lunch time meetings. Many times concerns will be raised at the meeting which have never been entered into the concerns resolution process. This allows items to be forgotten and to fester to become major issues, therefore it is mandatory that the concerns resolution process is seen as the proper tool to ensure issues are dealt with. At the end of the lunchtime meeting it is important that all concerns not in the system are captured and entered into the process, and you must follow up to ensure the item is introduced.

Opinion Gathering & Diagonal Slice Activities

Another important approach in the communication strategy is to structure activities to gather feedback from the workforce on various aspects of the business. This is not a casual open ended activity but is a focussed activity to ensure that necessary actions are taken to improve.

For small local projects lunchtime meetings for those affected can be arranged with a

specific agenda aimed at gathering opinions and feedback about progress.

Decisions can be taken after everybody's input and consensus is obtained. This is a very positive approach to ensure everybody remains aligned and actions are not taken against the well being of anyone in the group.

When dealing with company wide issues e.g. management behaviours, opinion polls can be used to measure the reactions of the workforce to what is happening. Results can be reviewed at department as well as company level.

Diagonal slice activities can be introduced to bring all levels of the organisation together to come up with a common policy and action to improve.

A diagonal slice activity brings people together from different departments and different levels of the organisation to consolidate understanding of an issue and find a common solution.

By engaging in diagonal slice activities you ensure the issue is considered from all perspectives (not only top managements) before the decision is made. If you ensure the decision is made through consensus of the complete diagonal slice group you will experience much more commitment to the action.

Diagonal slice activities are also beneficial when a company policy decision has to be implemented; in this case the focus is not on the decision but in finding the best method of implementing it.

Many companies with poor communications end up spending more time negatively debating with their trade unions the poor decisions handed down to the workforce sooner than working on the best solution.

Another form of opinion gathering is through the use of suggestions/feedback boxes where individuals can post their ideas or opinions on burning issues either anonymously or with their name on the form.

However if you use the methods described above normally the box will stay empty in favour of face to face communication.

In the past I have been frequently surprised how positively members of the workforce discuss even the most frustrating concerns if they know they are being listened to.

Remember communication is not just an action taken when you want to say something. It is a strategy which if carried out thoughtfully will provide you with :

- Information and insight about the real conditions in the workplace.

- Manager/member face to face communication as a part of daily business.

- Two way dialogue on removing road blocks to achieving company goals.

- An increased level of trust and support from the workforce.

- an improved ability to resolve concerns that are preventing achievement of company goals.

- more right first time decisions by encouraging all levels to participate.

- Complete focus on the important issues.

Actions

- Review your Company Communication Strategy to determine what it is trying to achieve (the list above should help)

- Structure your communication activities to include the above methods and ensure there is a process for reviewing progress.

- Educate your management team to enable them to adopt the methods, make particular reference to behaviours avoiding defensiveness particularly with the casual conversation opportunities.

- Use company opinion surveys to measure the progress the company is making in developing an open consultative type environment.

- Introduce diagonal slice meetings and activities to improve communication across the natural boundaries of the organisation.

Open Communication

8. Non – Monetary Reward & Recognition

Maslow's hierarchy of needs

To discuss non-monetary reward and recognition it is first important to consider the needs of humans and how they can fulfil those needs.

It is true to say that the vast majority of people go to work to earn money and provide security for themselves and their families.

But once these basic needs are fulfilled people's needs change or you could say develop.

To understand this, let's take a look at Maslow's "Hierarchy of Needs". As can be seen in the figure below (Fig. 16) as people achieve a level of needs so they automatically move up to the next level. Quite often

they do not realise this has happened. They just feel dissatisfied even though they have a well paid job and security.

They may even have good friends and experience, and very positive relationships, but something is missing.

Do people respect them and appreciate what they do?

How many times do you hear a mother who stays at home to look after young children say "No one notices what I do, I miss being appreciated for my work".

Well to be fair it's true, there is very little reward and recognition for doing the housework, is there?!

This can also be true of your workforce if you depend on the annual wage negotiation to express your appreciation, especially if you enter traditional negotiations where it seems the Trade Unions are trying to get blood out of a stone! (Perception is reality).

So how do we take the work force through this journey of satisfying their needs?

Fig. 16

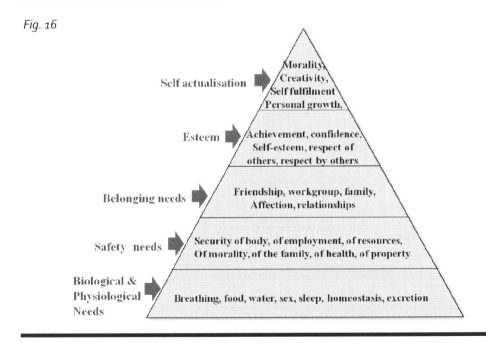

Managing People's needs at work

We assume that the people you employ are able to satisfy their basic biological and physiological needs.

To satisfy their safety needs, it is important that your benefits package provides adequately for job and family security. Your vision and outlook for the company looks positive and the health and safety of your workforce is taken care of.

You can now move them to the next stage by utilising team work and involving everyone in company decision making, demonstrating that they are trusted as part of the team. Consensus decision making, quality circles and diagonal slice activities also provide opportunities for people to feel they belong to a great company.

Once you have them locked into these activities, to satisfy their next set of needs you need to recognise their efforts and enhance their self esteem. Management behaviour in line with exemplary beliefs and values goes a long way to achieve this, but having a celebratory non-monetary reward and recognition system led by a truly appreciative management team really improves self esteem.

It is therefore important to separate reward and recognition from the money people take home in their pay.

People get paid for being in the team and for ensuring that their performance is competitive, so a person's pay should not be considered to be a reward. It is in fact remuneration for the service they provide to the company and is a right, not a reward.

Of course part of the pay increase should be based on the overall competitiveness of the company, but again this is not a reward, it is a just and fair sharing of the cost savings of the company.

So it is important if you want to stimulate pride that you have other ways of recognising good effort and success.

Types of reward & Recognition

In a company that believes in challenge it is important to recognise good effort even if full success has not been achieved. Frankly if the targets are truly stretching, then on occasions they will not be met and this will not be the fault of the workforce.

To keep morale high during a challenge activity a celebration should be held by management with the people involved. This should acknowledge the tremendous work done so far, recognise that we might not make the target and encourage everyone to keep trying so that we can get as close as possible.

The celebration should focus on what is being achieved not on the short fall,. Attendees must leave the celebration feeling that they have been thanked for their participation.

One of the best ways of doing this is to call for a group lunch with the buffet being supplied by management; top management as well as local managers should attend and offer their congratulations and thanks.

The managers should take their lunch side by side with the team and should mingle and have conversations with as many members as possible.

There are two aspects of daily activity that must take precedence over everything else. These are : the health and safety of the workforce and the maintenance of the highest possible quality standards in your products. Therefore it is crucial to encourage people to be always on the look out for anything that might compromise those two principles. They should be encouraged to report anything they consider to be a risk.

For any items that are found and corrected there should be recognition of the person who was so observant and celebration of avoiding a potential serious situation. In lean companies the person will be presented with a "Golden Eye" or "Good Citizen" plaque with their name and the date engraved on it. Depending on the degree of problem the plaque will be gold, silver or bronze.

The individual would also receive a gift from the company Public Relations memento catalogue. All of these awards would be presented at the end of the morning tea/coffee break (on a Friday) by a member of top management. For companies that do not have such catalogues an agreement with a local gift shop can work just as well.

A photograph of the presentation should be taken and it should appear in the next company newsletter giving another moment of recognition, company wide.

This combines the acts of recognition and reward and provides three mementos of the occasion. On talking to several recipients I have found them to be very proud of the award and in several cases there was an underlying competition for groups to be considered the best "Good citizens" of their department.

Other companies provide vouchers for an individual to take their partner out for a dinner in a nice restaurant. This is normally appreciated by the individual but is lower key recognition and there are only memories not mementos, unless they leave with the table cloth!

Success must always be celebrated!

Can you imagine winning in the Olympics or the World Cup in football and there being no medal ceremony or celebrations after the event?

Well a successful project completed is like the Olympics or the world cup for the team who achieved the task. How motivated will they feel if their success is ignored and not acknowledged?

Use simple awards such as a certificate for the team or group acknowledging the success. Add a cap or T-shirt with a logo for each participant to remind them of their success. Couple this to a free lunch celebration with the top management team, with a photograph in the company newsletter and you have very low cost reward and recognition.

There was one individual I knew who changed his holiday arrangements so as not to miss out on the celebration.

When asked "Why"?

He replied;

"There are very few occasions in this life when someone says "well done". I'm not going to miss this one"!

One very important point is to ensure that "busy" management do not miss a promised recognition ceremony ; it really turns the workforce off, even if it is some one else in the department who has been let down.

There are other ways to give reward and recognition:

Dispense free coffee and tea from the company vending machines for 24 hours after success of a company wide activity. Do not promise this, just make it a spontaneous decision on completion of the activity!

When an individual has led a change activity which can be used in other departments, free the individual up to present his activity to those departments and act as an advisor while they implement the same.

Japanese companies hold Quality Circle competitions in their plants and invite the winners of each plant to Japan to present their project and celebrate their success.

Allow individuals who have found quality defects in supplier parts to visit the supplier and present to the workforce what the impact of the defect is on the company and its customers.

Share free tickets to an industrial show (e.g. motor show) with the workforce instead of giving them to the management team exclusively.

By developing themes for Quality Circles and making the activity a company wide competition you can add to the competitive spirit of the company and if your recognition of all finalists is effective, motivation as well as self esteem will rise considerably.

Recognising events in your peoples lives

Another way to give recognition is to use a large notice board/monitor display in the entry to the workshop, personal success stories with photos and information on special events non- working as well as working.

Congratulations on someone's birthday (or birth of a child) can also be displayed ; this is another strong form of recognition, and the fact that the company remembers people's birthdates and celebrates is powerful as a motivator (and easy to do). In one company it was the habit of the team members and group leader to buy a birthday cake for the individual to share in the morning tea break.

For some this may all sound rather paternalistic and the cynics might say people only come to work for money, but I can truly assert that "It works".

People do like to be told what a good job they have done and that it is appreciated.

Thank you goes a long way! It is surprising how good you feel when you are leaving work and you pass your boss and he says

"Thanks for your efforts, it's been a good day".

Try the following actions and be surprised!!

83

Actions

- Review what actions are taken in your company to recognise good effort. Recognition should be given by departmental management and should be celebratory.

- Review what actions are taken to celebrate success. Ensure that recognition is immediate, that there is a memento and that it appears in the company newsletter for sharing with the recipient's family.

- Review what actions are taken to recognise when an individual notices a potential safety issue or quality defect. Ensure that recognition comes from top management, that there is a memento and that it appears in the company newsletter for sharing with the recipient's family.

- Ensure that these actions are supported by the total management team and that praise is considered by every one to be genuine.

- When you set the date and time for a recognition ceremony make it sacrosanct.

Reward and Recognition

9. The PDCA Management Cycle

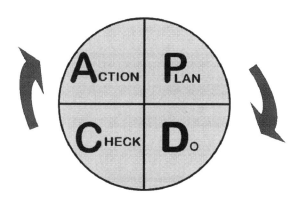

Fig. 17

"Making Plans Work"

An extremely effective Management tool for ensuring activities progress and deliver their required goal is called the PDCA management Cycle. When used properly it ensures continuity and a fast response to problems.

PDCA stands for Plan, Do, Check, Action and enables individuals or groups to follow activities from small concerns up to large projects, allowing each stage of the activity to have *Check/Action* cycles carried out on them. Thus during **Planning** a check cycle can be utilised to see if the planning is going to schedule and is focussed on the right objectives, if not, actions can be taken to correct the flawed plan.

During the **Do** cycle a check must be carried out to see if the Plan is being implemented as intended, if not action must be taken to come back into line or understand why the original plan will not work.

You would be surprised how many organisations fail to carry out what they say they are going to do. Then they are surprised when the planned results do not manifest themselves and they actually think the plan was no good!!

During the **Check** cycle it is important to ensure that the review is being carried out against correct and all criteria and that it identifies all shortfalls.

From the check phase may come some further **actions** to ensure all criteria are achieved. During this phase it is important to check that the results truly satisfy the requirements.

When they have achieved their aims, quite often management want to move on to the next challenge, little realising that unless all improvements are standardised they will not be sustainable. This manifests itself a few months later when the anticipated savings start to deteriorate giving the impression that the plan was no good.

To complete the **Action** phase all targets should be achieved, all changes must have been standardised and documented to prevent slip back, so the check on this phase must ensure this takes place.

I hope from this description it is clear that every phase of the PDCA must have a management review (check) carried out on it so that management guide the team to a successful conclusion.

In some organisations everything is left to carry on until the end of implementation, no one has noticed that the activity has drifted off target and out of control; individuals have been left on their own with many problems which all come to light when the objective is not achieved.

This dissatisfies everyone especially the people who have put lots of personal time into the project. If a review had been carried out at the planning stage and periodically during the subsequent phases these problems would have been identified and counter measured before they became a disaster.

PDCA should become the way of managing what is going on in the organisation; many managers say they are too busy to carry out PDCA but when you review their activities, much of it is trying to catch up with ongoing activities without any structured follow up. This wastes time as the manager tries to uncover what is happening. He has to find the latest plan (which is still out of date), find the people responsible, establish the progress milestones and assess whether this is really going to achieve the desired results in time.

Check questions by phase

If managers are going to empower their people to make decisions and implement them, the PDCA offers a method to follow the process and review (Check) at each stage, the following are the types of checks that need to be carried out in each phase:

PLAN

Do the individuals understand the goals and objectives to be achieved?

Is the plan practical?

Will the plan achieve the goals and objectives if carried out properly?

Is the plan being developed on time?

Is there a communication plan for the activity?

DO

Is the plan being carried out exactly as intended? If not why not? OK/Not OK?

If the change was necessary will the modified plan achieve the goals and objectives?

If the change was not necessary, what steps are being taken to get back on plan?

Are there any difficulties/concerns that need support?

Will the implementation be carried out on time?

CHECK

Are the goals and objectives being used to check the results?

Is a check being carried out for any remaining concerns?

If results are achieved are they sufficient to resolve the initial problem?

Are any other problems caused to others by the implementation?

ACTION

Was it necessary to take further actions?

Do we understand what didn't work as well as planned?

Are containment actions necessary while long term countermeasure is sought?

Is external knowledge or skill needed to assist finding a solution?

Has the change (when successful) been standardised?

It is important to recognise that the Action stage of PDCA can in effect become another PDCA cycle. One would hope that big actions are not required, but if any actions are taken they **mus**t be reviewed by PDCA. This is quite often where efforts trail off and results are never delivered because management move on to the next big thing!

At every stage, when a review is carried out, immediate action must be taken to correct a deficiency. Whether in planning or doing or checking nothing should be left hoping it will come good during implementation. It will not and the project will fail to deliver its expected results.

Advantages and applications of PDCA

Working to PDCA reduces the time that managers aimlessly walk the floor to "see what is happening". By structuring all activities in a PDCA format and scheduling reviews managers can keep people focussed on what should be happening (see Fig. 18 below for a typical PDCA format). But all reviews should take place on the shop floor where the activity is happening!

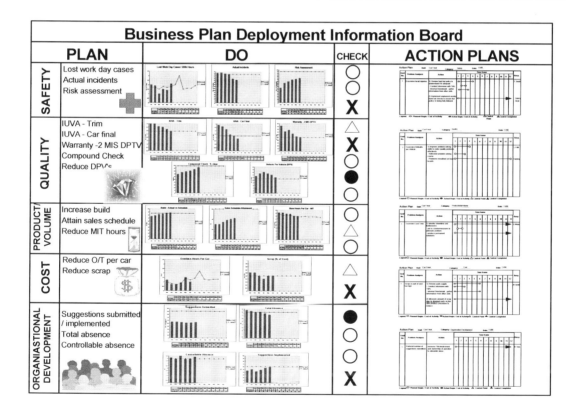

Fig. 18

Another common failing is not giving front line management the time to carry out daily performance reviews to properly follow what is happening,. Too often high level management meetings are called by the various departments and the unit manager hardly ever sees his production area.

In Toyota there were periods during the day when the unit manager was helped to follow activities in the work place; no one (including the M.D.) was allowed to call a meeting during these periods. The manager was expected to devote all this time to being on the shop floor, reviewing and supporting activities. Managers from other departments were expected to support shop floor activities during these times as no meetings were called then.

When activities are organised in a PDCA format using visual management, everybody understands their role, reviews are planned and take place with a given frequency, and management of the activity becomes simple and effective.

This allows managers to become leaders using the PDCA reviews to give praise for work done, guidance where plans are unclear, and support where difficulties are experienced, all in a timely manner so that project/activity milestones are not missed.

The PDCA management cycle can be applied to manage the following types of activity:

Business Plan progress – Health & Safety, Quality, Delivery, Cost, Development. Check monthly each areas progress and ensure actions are being taken if they fall behind.

Daily Operation performance – Quality and Delivery (schedule attainment)

Member concerns – management follow up

to give support and ensure difficult items are addressed.

Projects – e.g. line speed changes, equipment repair or improvement, model change, new equipment installations.

In fact anything that needs organising, make it a standardised way of life to assure progress.

Actions

- Review how your management team tracks progress of concerns or actions/projects.

- Set up a standard PDCA tracking process and train your managers.

- Agree with your managers how and when they will carry out reviews and give them the time to do it (do not allow meetings to be called during this period).

- Ensure your managers use the reviews to coach each stage of the action and give positive feedback where progress is good.

- Use PDCA reviews to identify where reward and recognition should be given to individuals or teams.

III. "Really" Involving People

10. Developing The Team

The primary rule to remember when endeavouring to become a highly competitive company is:

"You can not do it on your own".

So a key strategy for you to work on is how to develop the people who work for you, encouraging and enabling them to acquire knowledge and skills which they can apply to improve the business.

So who should you develop?

Training for Succession

To ensure good management development and continuity it is important to have a process for identifying and training the next team leaders, group leaders and managers.

As Toyota experienced, head hunter activities are far more prolific in the UK. Their managers were targeted due to their exceptional knowledge and skills, resulting in a higher than anticipated manager turn over. Therefore it was necessary for them to take steps to strengthen their management organisation.

It is necessary to have a succession and development plan for every management position, with at least two candidates for each position if possible.

Consideration should be given as to how all potential managers gain experience in the production management activity. After all this is where the revenue is generated.

Finance, human resources management support, engineering and material logistics all need to have a minimum of six weeks experience in production, to understand the complexity of the department so that they will be able to give more practical support.

Production group leaders should be selected from the team leader ranks. By doing this their knowledge of the production principles will be based on practical experience, not just theoretical learning.

Each candidate needs to have a strong knowledge of the production system principles, application of business plan deployment and consensus decision making, in order to be able to ensure performance improvement sustainability.

A newly promoted, unknowledgeable group leader can very quickly undermine performance of the group and allow the basic production and management principles to erode very quickly as good management practices lapse and bad practices take over.

Toyota experienced this situation in the UK during the early years of 2000. As the head hunters plundered them, group leaders had to be promoted with little experience and some new managers and group leaders were employed from outside with no Toyota Production System knowledge.

For several years they struggled with on the job training programmes. To counter the loss of experience, several production areas needed to go back to basics to re-align their activities.

But development is not only for Managers!

Most companies when they think of employee development only consider the 10-15% who are high potential, destined to become managers; they forget the power of having the other 85-90% applying their effort to make the company hugely successful.

Developing for success

Dynamic companies such as Toyota not only manufacture products, but also engage in continuous improvement of their operations to reduce cost and increase profitability every single day.

It is clear that Managers can not do this by themselves. There are comparatively few of them and they do not have the intimate knowledge of each of the manufacturing processes.

So these companies invest in their people. They ensure that each person understands not only how to carry out their process but also about the basic design concepts, particularly the principles behind avoiding waste in the process.

They are taught how to recognise waste in their process, how to remove it and reduce operating costs.

All changes to their processes have to be agreed by them and they are always involved in implementation of them.

All of this empowers shop floor workers to have a say in the way they perform their jobs, it also creates interesting tasks in addition to carrying out repetitive assembly operations.

Gone are the days when management wanted operators to leave their brains at the gate when they arrived for work.

Today the message must be clear that *"they are the most important resource the company has and the company is committed to spend money developing their skills and potential"*.

They are also taught how to recognise abnormalities (potential for defects or lost production). They are trained in Problem Solving skills so that they can countermeasure the abnormalities, thus avoiding defects and additional costs.

They are encouraged to get involved in the "5 aspects of manufacturing" helping to track and achieve the Business plan.

5 aspects of manufacturing: Health & Safety, Quality, Delivery, Cost Reduction & People Development.

They receive training in the department budgets, H&S, recycling, scrap & rework control, quality assurance, build scheduling etc. as they carry out activities to support the Business Plan.

Every member has the opportunity to learn new skills e.g. problem solving, process management, process improvement, total productive maintenance, Business Plan deployment etc.

The next generation of team leaders are identified and training is given on small group behaviours, roles and responsibility of team leaders and leadership activities for collecting data and solving problems. Training is also given in how to support their team members achieve first time quality through Andon systems and error proofing. They learn how to recognise and deal with potential ergonomic and health and safety problems using the synergy of their teams.

Practically all of the training is given in house with as much on the job as possible. Internal experts from various departments are used to carry out the training as these people are capable of demonstrating the practical use of the skills.

By utilising the workforce in this manner you unleash at least 20 times the power than if everything was left to the management team. Can you imagine the difference that makes to the bottom line?!

Training and development should not be sheep dipping exercises, but activities carried out as support for specific roles that the members will be carrying out. Therefore training is only given to attain a skill to carry out an activity.

This part of the book is going to deal with ways of involving the workforce in becoming the cost saving army of the company.

I will suggest several ways in which you can practically involve your people in taking responsibility for improving processes and general operations in the 5 aspects of manufacturing (Safety, quality, delivery, cost, and HR development).

Actions

- Determine the key elements of your production system and which skills need to be developed by whom. (Each level of the organisation will have different skill/ knowledge requirements.)

- Review your succession planning and ensure you have more than one candidate for each key role.

- Determine the level of training required to have a seamless hand over if a person decides to leave.

- Ensure the management team identify every individual with the potential to become the next team leader and a future supervisor and determine a development plan for them.

- Make sure that appraisal interviews include discussions on development, understanding the aspirations of the appraised person.

Developing the Team

11. Making Involvement Practical

It is in management's interest to provide an interesting and stimulating place to work, where everyday there is a feeling of making progress and that improvement is coming from the efforts of everyone.

Involvement cannot be passive ; people must carry out meaningful tasks specifically aimed at performance improvement which can be measured on the bottom line.

Part I of this book focussed on setting such a working environment in the company to create the opportunity to have a work force that feels it is an important and an integral part of the company.

In Part II of this book, the importance of everyone understanding their role and responsibilities was explained, in particular the role that the front line supervisor plays in encouraging the support and participation of the workforce. It was also stressed that giving recognition and feedback from all levels of management is important to the success of involving people.

So having set the scene and made clear the expectations, we need to have a means of converting all of that potential into action. There have to be tasks that people can perform in the knowledge that they are going to make a difference.

It is not reasonable to think that people will participate in activities "as instructed" by management, that is to say performing tasks as directed without understanding the principles of what is happening.

Therefore the tasks assigned to your people must be considered practical, important, and developmental; increasing the knowledge and skill of your people, as well as bringing success to the organisation.

The activities that they become engaged in must utilise their skills and give them responsibility for making decisions about the work they do.

The tasks should give them satisfaction and recognition for the contribution they are making towards the success of the company.

Following are some practical approaches that the company can take to achieve involvement of members in improving their knowledge and skills while at the same time contributing to performance improvement. Feel free to develop these ideas to provide opportunities that fit within your organisation's activities.

Primary Process Leader (PPL)

Normally in a production environment operators learn more than one process to provide flexibility within their working group e.g. to cover absenteeism.

One way to engage every person in the workforce is to give them responsibility for the condition of one of the processes they perform.

This process is called his "Primary Process" and no changes can be made to the process without the involvement of the PPL.

The PPL takes responsibility for the physical condition of the workstation including the tooling and equipment for that process.

They are charged with carrying out regular daily improvements to the process as well as ensuring everything is in good working order at the start and end of every working shift.

They carry out minor changes to the process to eliminate waste and make the process easier to perform; they also lead improvement activities with all the members that work on the process to generate a higher number of ideas for improvement.

In taking on this function they learn:

- The principles of good process design to avoid waste and to build in quality.

- How to standardise a process including documentation and training methods.

- How to eliminate waste in all of its forms.

- The control of quality assurance tooling (why it is important and how to do it).

- Practical Problem Solving skills.

- How to back up the process if equipment fails.

- Skills to enable manufacture of simple help devices.

- How to carry out "source inspection"*

*Source Inspection is a methodology used to review the process and parts design, looking for weak points in the design which may lead to difficulties and errors, therefore potential defects. This is a pro-active approach to seeking out abnormalities.

To assist the Primary Process Leader in his improvement activities the team leader carries out an audit of the process against the process design standards. This identifies which production principles need to be addressed to improve the design of the process.

This audit will not only help the PPL with ideas but will give him a measure of his improvement progress. If progress is faltering the team leader will help develop improvement ideas. If progress is slow due to lack of external support the difficulties will be identified through the concerns tracking system to solicit company support.

If the company operates two shifts there should be a PPL on each shift. They will operate a hand over log to communicate on activities or difficulties across shift. They will share the responsibility for all changes between them developing good team work across shifts.

Having experienced this activity in a plant, I was struck by how seriously the members took this role, the audits produced a score out of one hundred and groups/teams competed to have the highest process design score.

On a company wide basis the company recognised groups that made the most significant progress, and the highest ranking group (s) in the plant.

For model change or equipment improvement activities the PPL is the person who interfaces with the engineering groups and quality department for the process.

The PPL works with all members and the group leader to ensure the changes are in line with good process design and production system principles. He works with his opposite number across shift to ensure that consensus of everyone is reached before implementing changes.

With this approach members buy in and commitment to successful implementation will never be an issue.

Even across shifts with the application of "Business needs" and "consensus" decision making, differences of opinion are quickly resolved, because it is easily seen which idea creates the best process design score and therefore the greatest improvement.

Business Plan Group

Representative (BPGR)

An area of the business that is traditionally held "close to the chest" by management is managing the annual business plan or budget.

Managers have tended to view budget control as a purely management function, and actions are taken to prevent expenditure beyond a certain level, sooner than rethinking the process application, eliminating waste and therefore reducing the costs naturally.

There are also some concerns about resistance when talking about direct headcount numbers, this features more in a company that does not have a transparent employment policy.

But in a company that has determined how to manage the headcount/capacity issue there should be no reason not to be completely open with the workforce about the cost savings that need to be achieved.

In fact let's involve them in all 5 aspects of manufacturing: Health & Safety, Quality, Delivery, Cost and Human Resources Development. Help them to understand how the budget has been determined for each of these subjects and let them participate in activities to achieve the plan.

One way of doing this is to select 5 individuals from each group leader to represent the group in the 5 aspects of manufacturing. These individuals will help breakdown the targets to group level and will work with the group to develop ideas for achieving the business plan.

Let us use Health & Safety as an example:

The person selected as a representative for a group works with a core management team consisting of a senior group leader (BPD Leader) and two group leaders plus of course representatives from other groups.

They will all be supported by a member of the health & safety department who will train them in the pertinent health & safety regulations and give advice on specific issues.

The total group will meet at least two times a month either after work or in a lunch time session to track progress, capture ideas and receive any training necessary.

The BPGR works with the team leaders in his/her group to develop activities such as H&S audits, specific safety issue actions, and to ensure that data from the H&S department is being used effectively to identify high risk processes.

He will also assist in the pre-shift talks to explain health & safety issues or actions that have to be dealt with.

So you can see from this activity the BPGR will:

Receive training from external expert departments in specifics of the aspect chosen; H&S regulations, cost management, quality standards, recycling waste etc.

They will learn how to strategise, make action plans and track progress (PDCA) with management to achieve the targets in the plan.

They will act as a catalyst back in their group for generating and implementing action plans.

They will learn how their activities impact the bottom line of the company and gain understanding about why **cost** is the only variable in the profit calculation* that can really be attacked to give consistent improvement results.

*PROFIT = SALES (revenue) - **COST***

Problem Solving Leader

Any person who experiences a problem, be it an accident, near miss or a quality defect is expected to act as a problem solving leader to countermeasure against the possibility of a repeat of the incident.

The person takes on personal responsibility by leading the activity because he will understand the conditions that prevailed at the time of the problem. However the rest of the team will be involved to help identify what occurred out of standard. They will contribute by detailing how they manage the process. Between them they will identify what went wrong and agree the final countermeasure.

The problem solving leader will be coached by the group leader learning how to carry out practical problem solving and how to collect data to verify the countermeasure.

Health & Safety Auditor

Once per week every person is given the assignment of carrying out a Health & Safety audit on another team's workplace. This normally happens after the morning tea break when the operations are stopped for 5 minutes to enable this activity to be completed. The individual is expected to submit a suggestion to the responsible team to overcome the safety issue along with the observation.

This chapter has focused on how you can make involvement practical with development of individuals as the focal point while generating savings which will benefit everyone.

The next chapter will deal with how to develop "team activities" that utilise the skills they have been learning, thus forming a "can-do" winning organisation that is up for anything.

Actions

- Review the skill profile you would wish to develop in your workforce.

- Decide what activities will enable the workforce to practice these skills on a regular basis (start with the ideas above but look in your organisation for practical applications).

- Determine who the natural trainers and coaches are for these skills and in which department they work in.

- Develop an on the job methodology for giving this training including the means of practicing the skills to make improvement. (Train to fill a need, not just for the sake of training)

- Develop a follow and recognition system for the development stage of this activity.

- Implement with full management support providing the necessary resources.

Involvement
Tasks

12. Encouraging Involvement through team activities

Involvement and commitment to the company goals can be considerably enhanced by encouraging team activities that promote the sharing of knowledge and skills.

In many companies working groups are split into working teams and the company considers that it has introduced Team Work!

But in reality the only thing the team shares is carrying out the processes assigned to them. They learn each other's processes to cope with absenteeism and that is as far as teamwork goes.

Working teams

In a world class company, that is the starting point for teamwork, the team is encouraged to be the initiator of any problem solving activities for issues whether they are health & safety, quality defects, output issues etc...

The team leader leads the problem solving activity with his team, collecting data and going through the practical problem solving process with them. The team leader is coached by the group leader.

The team collects data about the occurrence e.g. a quality defect. Data will be used to determine which process the defect occurs on, which member was on the process, the type of defect (part missing, operation not completed, completed but out of standard).

Using this data they determine if a member needs retraining, or if a process has a particular difficulty that affects everyone. They then identify the appropriate countermeasure as a team and support the implementation.

In this way an individual never gets blamed or left on his own with a problem ; the team supports until the problem is fully resolved.

When it is discovered that the issue needs support from an external group the concerns resolution process takes effect and the group leader invites other people to join the team and support them.

Through the use of the concerns tracking process, support resources are drafted in by management as required, expanding the team size, and everyone focuses on resolving the issue.

Improvement Teamwork

Teamwork also spreads through the efforts of trying to improve processes. Not only does the team support the Primary Process Leader, but small working groups are also formed when necessary to build any required assembly aids.

The working group (kaizen groups)* includes operators, engineers and maintenance personnel. This activity spreads teamwork out across departments, skill sharing takes place and better working relationships are developed.

Kaizen groups– typically Japanese- consists of maintenance people and potential production team leaders who manufacture assembly aids working with the production teams.

These working groups are encouraged to develop skills such as welding, use of pneumatics and hydraulic circuitry and basic mechanical assembly.

The trainers are members of the maintenance and engineering groups who teach and coach specific assembly aid manufacture.

Typical assembly aids provided by these groups are man mover platforms, battery driven automatic guided vehicles, lifting/manipulation aids, guides and fixtures.

These groups can work in a number of ways:

1. In some cases the company recognises the need for continuous improvement and therefore builds into the headcount a number of people to staff the improvement teams. Needless to say the number of people added to the headcount determines the "minimum" savings that the improvement team must generate per year to pay for their existence and guarantee improved bottom line performance year on year.

2. Maintenance teams prepare the required equipment during the shift and production team members join them on overtime to progress the work and be trained in various skills.

3. Weekend and after shift overtime is used to bring the improvement teams together to work on the assembly aids.

Back-up Teams

For processes which utilise assembly equipment, back-up teams are formed comprising of production operators, engineers, maintenance, materials logistics and quality assurance departments.

The back-up team led by the production senior group leader determines what must be done to keep production flowing if the equipment fails.

They detail the actions that each member of the back-up team will take, itemising any additional aids required. If possible the aids will be manufactured by the team.

The team carry out occasional dry runs, periodically checking aids and methods to ensure everyone knows what is required of them.

When the equipment fails maintenance quickly assess whether back-up is necessary and if so the senior takes over organising everyone to come and support.

He calls the external members to come immediately to the line, to put the back up plan into action; this takes preference over any other work they might be engaged in.

A live log is kept by the senior of all of the issues and actions taken to countermeasure them. The log is recorded on a large display board so that team members can add comments as the actions progress.

During the backup activity, management visit the activity to give support, recognition and encouragement to the team, sometimes assisting them in parts of the process to share the load.

When the emergency is over, the back up team analyses the situation using the log to see what permanent countermeasures can be implemented to avoid a repeat of the problem. They also identify what can be improved in the back up process in case another issue arises at a later date.

In addition to this they identify how much product was lost due to the problem and how much would have been lost if there was no back up. Continuous improvement thinking is applied to see if the loss can be reduced next time and a celebration takes place recognising how much product was saved.

The back up team activity generates a real sense of working together to benefit the bottom line and therefore the future of the company.

In many companies this does not happen, production stops until maintenance repair the equipment, then starts up again, usually after considerable lost production.

The back up teams learn:

- The critical aspects of the equipment in their workplace and the interface points between human worker and machine.

- How to substitute human activity in place of the machine during emergencies.

- How to identify the critical quality points of the process for ensuring the back-up process maintains quality.

- How to plan and test and train an activity.

- Skills for making production aids.

- How team work can be used to reduce the impact of equipment failures.

Quality Circle Teams

The formation of quality circle teams is used to tackle more complex problems that will need extensive data collection, external support and investigation from more than one point of view.

The problems tackled are business issues and performance constraints as well as quality issues.

Cross functional teams are brought together to work their way through the problem using a structured approach to practical problem solving.

Some Japanese companies consider this activity to be so important they set aside 30 minutes per month where production in the plant is stopped to allow the teams in the plant to accelerate progress.

In addition to the 30 minutes the teams are expected to meet either during lunch times or after work on overtime. The team will be led by the initiator of the concern who will be coached by his group leader to ensure a sound approach is taken to the problem solving.

Some companies also add a competitive edge to find the best Quality Circle activity not only through its result, but also considering the approach taken and the amount of learning the group achieved.

As a prize, the winning group gets to visit company headquarters to celebrate their success and participate in an international forum to present and discuss the various projects.

Diagonal Slice Teams

The use of diagonal slice teams to tackle organisational or behavioural issues is a very powerful tool for gaining consensus while improving morale and trust.

Leading companies use this approach when they have carried out an opinion poll about management behaviours and discovered that the workforce is not satisfied.

Bringing together people from all levels and departments of the organisation to work on the issues ensures that all view points are considered and that learning from the activity is spread within the organisation.

Forming diagonal slice working groups is particularly suited for company wide issues where there is more than one point of view to be considered before making a decision. It is particularly beneficial when the solutions available are not going to be well received by all parties.

The diagonal slice group ensures that all view points are considered and that none are brushed aside. The "perceived loser" of the decision will at least know that the decision was the best of the alternatives and a good working relationship will have been formed. This leads to more trust in the company even when tough decisions are being made.

It must be realised that diagonal slice activities may slow down the decision making process. However when the decision has been taken you will normally experience a much faster and more successful implementation phase.

Under no circumstances should diagonal slice activities be undertaken if management are not sincere about listening and giving proper consideration to everybody's input. Only doing it for show will not only slow your decision making down but will have a negative impact on implementation.

Actions

- Consider what business processes in your organisation would really benefit from cross-functional team working.

- Identify the tangible benefits expected and identify the resources (training, trainers, support groups etc.) needed to achieve a successful outcome.

- Start with one pilot group to create the model for the organisation, take the time to de-bug any issues, and then roll out the process as quickly as possible.

Team Activities

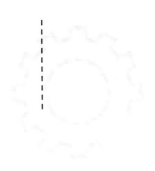

In writing this book I have endeavoured to describe as plainly and briefly as possible the conditions, behaviours and practices that will enable the application of the Lean Tools to thrive.

The visual management charts and process descriptions I have included allow supporting activities to be introduced with minimum preparation.

In all probability there are a number of companies that employ some of these tools for major projects or when they are experiencing a major problem. But these practices are most effective when they are applied to everyday business, and if used as such, will develop a very strong and capable organisation.
By applying these practices, you will be building a strong foundation on which the business will grow stronger day by day.

Although these practices are easy to understand, they take a lot of courage and determination to initiate. They are not for the mildly interested or the faint hearted. They are for those who have the staying power to drive a successful company and are willing to put faith in their workforce to achieve it!

So, before you put this book down, decide which actions you are going to take straight away to start the change process.

You could start with communication. Introduce lunch box meetings and listen to what your people think. Mix them with diagonal slice discussions and learn how well the different levels/parts of the company get on.

You could also use them to improve the understanding and inter-reactions between the levels and parts of the organisation.

Start following concerns and their resolution, introducing an escalation process when appropriate.

There are lots of things you can do in preparation before you have formulated your vision. Choose your research team to study the Lean Tools : managers, trade unionists, technical experts and team members, and let them start developing some expertise.
You do not have to wait. There is no time like the present and the sooner you start the sooner you will reap the benefits.

About the Author

John Hurst was born in the UK in 1949. He has worked for 40 years in the Auto industry for General Motors and finally Toyota.

He worked his way from apprentice engineer through the ranks of management to a top management position.

On the way he had several interesting assignments including a period as General Motors Europe- Director of manufacturing Quality Network implementation.

Quality Network was the name given to GM's lean production system.

John led a team which worked with all 15 Opel and Vauxhall Motors Manufacturing Plants across 8 countries in Europe in developing the strategy and rolling out lean practices.

Following this assignment he was transferred to the Opel Technical Development Centre in Germany to implement lean practices and stimulate plant involvement in the vehicle development process.

Finally in 1996 John returned to the UK as Works Manager of the Vauxhall Motors Ellesmere Port vehicle assembly plant until his retirement from Vauxhall Motors in 2003.

Later in 2003 John was approached by Toyota UK to carry out a three year assignment in their Burnaston Plant where after all the years of struggling to implement lean the light came on.

John says:

"I want to share the learning from my experiences both positive and negative in a way that answers the question of why companies that copy lean principles do not get the results they seek and what can be done to solve the puzzle".

"I hope this book achieves that aim"

Selected References

- Toyota Production System Beyond Large Scale Production
  Taiichi Ohno

- Non-stock production : The Shingo system for continuous improvement
  Shigeo Shingo

- Zero Quality Control: Source Inspection & Poka-yoke system
  Shigeo Shingo

- Just in Time For Today and Tomorrow
  Taiichi Ohno with Setsuo Mito

- Out of the crisis
  W. Edwards Deming

- A revolution in Manufacturing: The SMED System
  Shigeo Shingo

- TPM Development Program
  Seiichi Nakajima

- TPM The Western Way
  Peter Willmot

- Kaizen
  Masaaki Imai

- Hoshin Kanri—Policy Deployment
  Yoji Akao

- Productivity Through Process Analysis (IE for the Shop Floor1)
  Junichi Ishiwata

- Productivity Through Motion Study (IE for the Shop Floor2)
  Junichi Ishiwata

Lean Tools

- 5S (work place organisation)
- Kaizen (elimination of waste)
- First Time Quality
- Practical Problem Solving
- Business Plan Deployment
- PDCA Management
- Visual Management
- Poke yoke (error proofing)
- Bottle neck Management
- Total Productive Maintenance
- Single Minute Exchange of Dies (quick change over)
- Lead Time Reduction
- Process Diagnostics
- Standardisation

BOOKS on LEAN MANUFAC-TURING

INDEX

ILLUSTRATIONS & CHARTS INDEX